HOW TO
WIN FRIENDS,
KICK ASS
& INFLUENCE
PEOPLE

HOW TO
WIN FRIENDS,
KICK ASS
& INFLUENCE
PEOPLE

Lynne Russell

St. Martin's Press ☙ New York

Library of Congress Cataloging-in-Publication Data

Russell, Lynne.
    How to win friends, kick ass & influence people / by Lynne Russell.
        p.   cm.
    ISBN 0-312-24403-7
    1. Russell, Lynne.   2. Women television journalists—United States
Biography.   3. Television news anchors—United States Biography.   4.
Television broadcasting of news—United States.
I. Title.
PN4874.R77A3   1999
070'.92—dc21
    [B]   99-36061
                                                                CIP

First Edition: November 1999

10   9   8   7   6   5   4   3   2   1

This book is dedicated to
women everywhere who believe in
relying on themselves first.

Acknowledgments

My love and everlasting gratitude to my father and mother for so many gifts. Thanks to Michael Solomon for his encouragement, Jeff Cohen for listening, and my agent, Craig Nelson, for his invaluable help and this great title. Thanks to the dear sisters whose names you'll find inside, along with Kimberley, Jennifer, Trish, Linda, Shoshana, and Inci for sharing their secrets. Thanks also to Keith Flannigan, P.I., for being my friend and mentor, and my instructor, Marshall Pereira, for teaching me how to kick ass!

Contents

Who the Hell Is Lynne Russell, and Why Is She Writing This Book?

Glad you asked. I never bought into the traditional roles assigned to women. It just never happened. I remember when I was ten years old someone gave me a big picture book titled, *You Could Be*; and it was for girls. I learned I could be a nurse or a secretary, a mother or a flight attendant, a dental assistant or a teacher. When I was asked which one I would choose, I chose none of the above. Every one of those careers is a respected undertaking, but even at ten I knew that none of them was me; and I did not feel compelled to oblige adults by limiting myself to the choices I was handed. Eventually I went to nursing school because I like the concept of solving mysteries and I think the human body is the most fascinating mystery of all, and because I genuinely wanted to help other people; but I wasn't emotionally cut out for it. As for motherhood, I loved it when it happened, but I never was a little girl who wanted *only* to live in a house with a picket fence and be a wife and a mother when I grew up. It just seemed to me that that was something you *also* did while you did something else. So you can imagine what it was like for little boys who played "house" or "doctor" with me. We always were fighting over the stethoscope and who got to say, "Honey, I'm home."

I firmly believe that lots of girls felt as I did. Now, as adults, we still harbor a desire to go deeper into being our own person. For me, this has meant taking on other challenges when I'm not on the CNN Headline News set.

Not that it wasn't challenging enough just getting to CNN. First came several years in radio back in the 70s, beginning with four years of spinning out the hits when the hits were still on vinyl; our ultra-small-size radio market—the college town of Fort Collins, Colorado—was the last to get them from the record companies. Also the FCC required my radio station to reduce transmitter power to only 500 watts at sunset, so we were lucky if they could hear us across the street; but the newness of the experience, the freedom to create, and the cast of characters (employees right out of the TV series *WKRP in Cincinnati)* made it all worthwhile. Then came seven years of hosting morning drive-time talk radio in Miami, which translated to rising well before the crack of dawn to referee political free-for-alls and convincing celebrities to drag their sleepy butts into the studio at 6:00 A.M. with the rest of us; otherwise they weren't going to get to promote their new books/diets/fragrances. This left afternoons for lying on the beach and continuing the quest for the perfect piña colada. Unless, as often happened, we were in a panic for a last-minute guest for the next morning's broadcast; in such a case, I was back wandering the hippie haven of Coconut Grove with my little Sony tape recorder, looking for the Hare Krishnas. We knew they always were good for an hour of colorful interviews, with unintelligible chanting in the background. Talking with them in their natural habitat beat inviting them to the station; after they'd been there for a morning, the men's john smelled like strawberries for a week. We never could figure out if it was incense or aftershave.

And I did a brief DJ stint at an FM rock station in Jacksonville, Florida. My then husband (the second), the brilliant and notoriously mild-mannered rock'n'roll radio programmer Jim Dunlap, was my boss. And that went rather well until the day I found I had to drop a piece of music from my show to make the timing come out right, and I opted to eliminate a Bee Gee's song. Jim heard it in his office, and *I could hear him* coming down the hall. Next thing I knew, he had put his fist through the control room door and had broken his hand. And I knew two things: He was not so mild-mannered, and the TV news offer I'd just received was going to save our marriage. As it turned out, Jim and I were together for eighteen years until we agreed to go our separate ways; in all that time he never attacked another door. He did provide me with wonderful years of laughter and spontaneity, shared confidences, exposure to great rock music, limo rides with stars, and his endless DJ one-liners, which never failed to crack me up because of the way he delivered them.

My radio days were followed by that television news anchor job in Jacksonville and others in Honolulu, Hawaii, and San Antonio, Texas. By the time I got to CNN, I couldn't even remember all the call letters of all the stations where I'd worked—never mind the network affiliations—which to this day always are changing.

Once I settled in at CNN, I found that although I loved my job, my devotion to journalism wasn't enough to make me feel fulfilled as an individual who was inquisitive about so many things. I needed to augment it with other interests. The ensuing few years have brought two black belts in the Korean-American street-fighting martial art of Choi Kwang Do, certification in open-water SCUBA diving, acting as bodyguard to folks who don't want to get their Armanis all wrinkled as they fend off friend and foe, deputy sheriff and certified Jail Officer, licensed private investigator, foreign-language student, and enthusiastic if clumsy ice hockey skater. The unconventional odyssey is continuing, despite the people who think I'm nuts for giving in to this restless nature; but I think they've got their feet in wet cement and they'd better get the hell moving before the stuff freezes them in place. *Aren't they even curious?*

I wanted to write this book to share these thoughts with you, because I believe that every woman has it in her to lead a more fulfilling life, with the gifts and opportunities she is given—whatever they are. I am the first to admit that many of the new areas I've explored just sort of happened to me, rather than the other way around. And that, in itself, is a lesson on being open to opportunity. There are months—years—when you are not open to new opportunities at all. Then suddenly you have more time, or are bored, or are just feeling rebellious and fed up with the way things are going . . . fired up to break away and do something on your own. And you jump right in and try something new. The trick, for all of us, is to remember that the opportunities are there whether we're in the mood or not. Think of it as a twelve-months-a-year clearance sale; you may not be in the mood to shop, but you really ought to just stop by and see what's there, in case you might be interested.

I hope that as you read this book you will be inspired to make as much of your days as you can, taking on any extra elements that give you a special thrill. I hope you will see that you must be true to yourself, asking yourself at every stage what *you* want to do with your life. Forget what you think you ought to do. What are you good at? What makes you happy? I hope you will gain the confidence to trust yourself and your intuition: the confidence to believe what you feel, even if there is no substantial, material evidence to support it. And I hope you will take to heart what Eleanor Roosevelt said about self-image. When I was twelve, my mother didn't go a day without quoting Eleanor. It drove me nuts; but this one is worth remembering: "No one can make you feel inferior without your consent." That one has stayed with me over the years. And as this geeky, scrawny twelve-year-old girl became a full-grown woman, I cared less and less what other people thought of me. Gradually, I embraced the delicious concept of not waiting another moment to partake, each day, of what life has to offer. And I developed.

Lynne's Rules

Rule 1: No Limits. Do not permit other, less-enthusiastic, less-imaginative, less-adventurous (and perhaps resentful) people to place limits on the effort you are willing to put forth to accomplish the things you believe you are able to achieve. I'm not necessarily talking about bungee jumping. Maybe you just always have had a yearning for volunteering at a hospital, or learning to build things, or nightclub singing, or breeding Chihuahuas. Go for it. What's the worst that can happen? They can't shoot you. (Well, that depends on your singing. There's a little-known statute in Chicago . . .)

Rule 2: Taste Lots of Things in Life. If you are blessed with the time, the ability, and the resources to learn to do even one more thing with the gifts God gave you, you are out of your mind if you don't get out there and see what's waiting for you. Taste this and taste that. It doesn't have to be a lifetime commitment. You can try it today and abandon it tomorrow. If you hang on to it, good for you. Amass as many experiences— even as many responsibilities—as make you feel good. Even if you let any of them go, you still will have learned something and will have expanded your universe. You owe it to yourself to try. Just remember: Whatever you do, it's supposed to be fun.

Rule 3: There Is Nothing Wrong with This World That Twenty Minutes in Victoria's Secret Won't Fix. *Politics.* If Hillary Clinton had had a hotline to Vicky's Secret, one wonders whether Monica Lewinsky ever would have gotten those private skin flute lessons in the Oval Office that prompted international debate over marital fidelity, presidential morality, and what constitutes a really stupid waste of television air time.

War. If Saddam Hussein had gotten the Victoria's Secret

end-of-season sale preview catalog, and had ordered a few little nothings for the ladies in his life (or maybe for himself, who can say; I can see him in a little black chiffon thing with thick maribou trim to match his mustache), maybe our troops wouldn't still be shaking sand out of their shorts. Comedian George Carlin characterizes war, in his stand-up routine, as nothing more than a "dick waving contest."

World Hunger. Let's get some after-hours private-shopping privileges and personal tea-room modeling invitations out to the world's wealthiest power brokers. Sure, they have so much money they can have anything they want any day of the week, but this is something different. It's the girl-next-door in lingerie they dream about. And a grateful boy will do just about anything to say "thank you," even slip some cereal to Sudan.

A bad day at the Office or the Altar. For the average woman, a good lingerie shop is a better fix than a box of warm, fresh-baked chocolate chip cookies *and* a plate of Death by Chocolate, if she'll just let herself get into it. It used to be that the first thing a woman did when she split from her man was to get a new hairdo. Why? You liked it before, so leave it alone. Go try on something that makes you feel fabulous. Try on lots of things. Try on so many things that the salesgirl who stands outside the fitting room has to count them all over again. You don't have to buy everything. Just see how great you can look—and go home with the one that says "fuck you" the best.

These are a few of the delicate, little feminine thoughts I've shared with women coast to coast, during my speeches and appearances, and in phone conversations and letters. We all seem to want basically the same things out of life; it's just a matter of figuring out how to get them by making the most of what we've got. And that just naturally is going to require shaking up a few people and their ideas. *It's going to require change.*

39 Signs You Need Change

The only thing that's sure is change. And that's great, because it keeps things that already are good from going stale, and it gets rid of the things that are causing your mental spool to unwind. We all need change, but we don't always know it, which causes us to waste our time resisting it. So here's a handy little guide to start you thinking. You know you need change in your life if:

1. As you walk down the street, strangers remind you of movie actors and actresses you haven't thought of in years.
2. You look at your coworkers and marvel at their resemblance to Walter Slezak and George Carlin, and those are just the women.
3. The urge to jump up and down on a pew during church service, making screeching monkeylike sounds, is becoming too attractive to resist.
4. You giggle as you read the hardware ads.
5. You used to tell people off in the shower, now they tell you off.

6. You see symmetry in piles of dirt.
7. You wail "Nothing good lasts forever" at weddings, and "Thank God for new beginnings" at funerals.
8. Your mate spends an extra thirty minutes on foreplay, to which you reply, "Smart-ass."
9. Objects appear closer than they are.
10. If you stare long enough at a word, it looks foreign.
11. You dream you got up to go to the bathroom during the night, but awaken in a wet bed.
12. You take the dog's medicine by mistake and feel better.
13. You imagine the ways one drop of superglue could change the world.
14. You feel an unnatural exhilaration when the garage-door opener works.
15. You chew gum because you can.
16. Birds are demanding answers.
17. You are mesmerized by the swirling waters of a flushing toilet.
18. Elevator music is too jarring.
19. When you are at home and the local directory-assistance operator asks "What city?" you don't know the answer.
20. You trace your hand at staff meetings, then sign and date it.
21. Santa tells you to clean up your act.
22. Alone in the dentist's waiting room, you notice magazines are moving.
23. Alone in the park, you think it odd that objects are not falling from the sky.

24. At least twenty minutes of each day is unaccounted for.
25. You regard the floor with new respect.
26. Your Caller ID is trying to fool you.
27. Every one-liner from *Casablanca* applies to you, especially, "I was misinformed."
28. Jack Kennedy calls.
29. You crack yourself up.
30. Someone catches you talking to yourself in the car, and you spend the next ten minutes continuing the conversation, or pretending you are singing, to throw him off.
31. You understand *everything* now.
32. Your face cream has turned on you.
33. You visit another country and marvel at how well the children speak the language.
34. You stand in front of the microwave and yell, "Faster!"
35. As you walk on a plush carpet, you smooth it behind you to cover your tracks.
36. When other people speak to you, you try to read their lips.
37. In a meeting with your boss, his voice fades in the background as you *will* his pants to split.
38. The froth in your cappuccino is spelling out a message.
39. You can answer your cell phone without finding it.

You can identify with some of these. Good! So can the rest of womankind. Just don't let some wise guy convince you that women are instigators of change only because our hormones play tag once a month. If you've ever wasted your precious time explaining to a man something that's bothering you, only to have him ask you if you're premenstrual, you know what I mean.

The Power of PMS

Some people like to say that women feel they need change only at "that time of the month." Well guess what, PMS does not stand for premenstrual syndrome. It stands for Pissed and Mercurial (but Sane). We just have a lower tolerance for bullshit. For instance, we've all been here:

There's nothing like sharing a close, loving relationship with a man you adore. One of the most comforting aspects is that you get to know each other so well, you can almost read each other's mind and you can tell without asking what the other person needs. A woman who learns to "read" her man finds that the signals he sends tend to be quite consistent. If he likes to retreat to a place where he can be alone for a while when he comes home from work, he'll probably feel the same way about it tomorrow or three weeks from now as he does today; that's okay because we need our space too. And if it is his habit to listen patiently to you as you air some concern, whether or not he does anything about it or even absorbs what the hell you're saying, he'll probably be exactly the same with that two weeks from now as he is today. Men tell me they handle things this evenly because they genuinely like it this way and, more important, because they consider it the safest route out of the minefield.

Not so for the female of the species. This consistent behavior we've come to expect from men makes it easier for us to deal with them. But men, those adorable, unsuspecting creatures of habit, are never quite sure which track our train is running on. They may blame this on hormones, but they need to remember that these are the same hormones that make us so damned interesting to them when they're "in the mood." As women, our natural quick wit and charm make us prone to consider each new situation as something we've never encountered before, which deserves fresh treatment. This can lead any conversation into uncharted territory and that's fine, because we know that men like a challenge and we are happy to oblige.

Now here's the problem: for the one week or so before our period every month, we are even more likely to handle things differently on a personal level. *Personal,* not business. We women are experts at setting priorities at the office and recognizing the times when we are apt to be less enthusiastic about a certain employee or less tolerant of a colleague with a different point of view, and we deal with it. About the only time I can recall even mentioning the time of the month at work, was the evening I was paying for my selection in the CNN cafeteria I call Chez Ted (officially known as the Hard News Cafe), when the cashier inquired how I was and I blurted out in front of everyone in line, "Thank you for asking. Actually, I'm premenstrual and I fluctuate between love for all mankind and the urge to hurl these mashed potatoes right up against that goddamn wall." Generally, it is a smart thing to wait until we get home to be so open—home, with our close friends and family, people less likely to E-mail the news around the world. And with them we are so much more honest about this particular week's revelations. We say exactly what we're thinking, without filtering it through the brain zones marked Diplomacy, Better Timing, and Sensitivity. In essence, we all become like my Italian half, with a direct line from Reaction Central to our mouths. This revelation is nothing new; the danger to our gender lies in its predictability.

If you are physically intimate with a man and he can read a calendar, he has a conversational advantage that you do not have. It can take you years to figure this out unless he says something that gives it away. He knows exactly when you're premenstrual, which means he knows when you're most likely to tell it like it is and least likely to calmly sit through a lengthy explanation of why he was two hours late getting home because he ran into his high school sweetheart at the grocery store and they discussed nothing more than the senior-year homecoming game. Yeah, right, probably halftime behind the bleachers. I've got your trip down memory lane, right here.

But there's more. Men think that when we say things they find unsettling during those Seven Dangerous Days, they are thoughts the devil has put there, which we could not possibly mean, and so they tend to discount them all. They need to know that sometimes there's something really important in there that's coming out now only because of that brain shunt that bypasses the filtering zones. The world is filled with broken hearts and shattered dreams because men didn't listen—they thought women were having an Estrogen Moment. So it is up to us to get the message across in the most diplomatic way. The things we say require editing and reediting so that they are not misunderstood by the gender we alternately love and hate.

I do not recommend voice mail, and I'll tell you why. I've tried it, and it hardly ever works out the way I want it to. It may seem like the least confrontational approach, and you may honestly believe that the words you have chosen so carefully are kind and show the consideration and respect you want to convey. But you just can't control *the sound of your voice*, and what it says can send a completely different message, one that would make you go out and rip up park benches if things were different and you were on the receiving end. You leave the sweetest voice mail, "Honey, I just want you to know that I see how you feel and I will try to be more understanding in the future. You are so dear to me and you don't have to worry, I really do believe that you mean it when you say you love me. I'll be here whenever you want to call, so we both can feel better." And he hears, "Listen to me, you cretinous sonofa-bitch, I'm world-class pissed, disgusted, and ready to rip your heart out. If you're a man in love, then I'd rather sit in the Seventh Circle of Hell with Jeffrey Dahmer. And if you don't call back before the moon rises, you aren't going to *believe* what happens next." Which is exactly what you wanted to say. The worst part is that once you hang up the phone and the betraying sound of your voice echoes in your head, you realize you may have made a serious miscalculation; but there's no going back. Any minute now Jeffrey Dahmer will call with your reserved seat.

The Lioness in You . . . or How I Learned to Fire a .357, and So Can You

The first time I got married I was nineteen. I would have married Charles Manson to get a little freedom. This guy was a "Southern Gentleman" who believed that since his mama picked up after him, *I* should relish the task. His grandfather had been a member of the Klan. I was an Italian Catholic who had grown up in a police-the-area-*now* army household. Can you see where this is going? I remember very clearly standing in the back of the army base chapel as I took my father's arm, thinking to myself, "Well, there's always divorce." The modern translation is, "Lynne, are you out of your fucking *mind*?"

If I had trusted my own instincts, I would have found another way to get a life, sparing all of us the turmoil of the next four years, of which I can remember exactly six days. The mind mercifully buries marriages-from-hell and other domestic debacles in that portion of the brain labeled "Unnatural Disasters." Even if it was partly my fault because I saw it coming, I can't help believing that if there is a God in heaven, the man who furnished me with all those barefoot-and-pregnant night-sweats in a trailer out in the Colorado countryside is sitting somewhere back home in his family's native Arkansas in some crocheted and quilted double-wide with a satellite dish and a six-pack of Pabst Blue Ribbon, pulling a Camel out of the pocket of his T-shirt and breathing hard from the exertion, pondering what might have been if he only had worked out the meaning of "get a job."

Let me tell you how this adventure went. We'd been married three months when he joined the National Guard to keep from going to Vietnam, and he went off to boot camp. He came back home for a Christmas visit and when he departed again to serve the rest of his duty, he took off with his military orders (the crucial papers that identify you and indicate where you are next assigned and when you must report) sitting on the closet shelf. In thirty years in the army, my father never left anything that important behind, and I should have known right then that this was going to be a culture clash. A couple of weeks later my husband was on the phone complaining about the living conditions in the barracks, suggesting he was ready to bail out, which of course he couldn't, because it was so "depressing." I was horrified by what I was hearing and grateful that my father—whom I had watched all my life spit-shining his shoes, polishing his brass, and dutifully doing the bidding of men of superior rank but inferior intelligence be-cause he had made the commitment and felt pride in what he did—who was watching me during this phone call, could not read minds or lips.

When the army turned my new husband loose from active duty and he came back home, it was agreed that although we both had some college left, we would move to his university town so he could finish school first. Ever the optimist, I ignored that little voice in my head yelling, "Idiot! Can't you see this guy can't even dress himself?" In four years, while I worked six days a week, he attended one quarter of college. And if work didn't find him, he didn't go looking for it. There's a moral to this story every few sentences: If you meet a guy in the lunch line at school and think his green eyes are really cool, and are impressed that his testosterone has kicked in well ahead of his peers (neither of which is anything *he* did) and date him for four years but don't live with him or even do a surprise inspection where he hangs out, don't expect to be thrilled with the results. You probably do more homework when you buy a car than I did with this one. It was just one, long date gone awry, but it certainly was a learning experience.

Another early clue that this was going to be a misadventure like you read about: his gray matter was scrambled. No, really. I know I can't stop other people from engaging in the "sport" of hunting, no matter how hard I try. They have their arguments and I have mine, and discussion is a waste of time for both of us. But an intelligent hunter can handle the annual event with a bit of finesse when the subject comes up. In our second year of bliss, he took off on a hunting trip and after three days returned triumphantly late one night to our cozy little twelve-wide trailer with a dead bird. In nervous anticipation of his arrival, and in dread of what bloody trophy he might be bringing with him, I couldn't sleep so I went to the living room to lie on the couch. And in he walked with this bird. As he began working it over in the kitchen sink, pulling out feathers and digging buckshot, I asked him if that was all.

Not eager for an altercation with a budding animal-rights activist—and way too friendly with Jack Daniel's on this trip to be a good debate opponent anyway—he turned around, looked me square in the eyes and with an absolutely straight face said, "Yeah. I didn't mean to kill it. I ran over it with the truck."

In the four years of that ill-fated mismatch, I began to see quite clearly that if he was against something, it probably was very good for me and promoted my independence. So I signed up for the free self-defense courses the police department was offering. The sadder his expression, when I came home from a full day's work at a dress shop and plopped a pot pie on the TV tray on my way out the door, the surer I was that I was headed in the right direction. The first thing they taught us was *aikido*—clever little ways to bend a person's thumb to get them to let you go. I used to lie in bed and fantasize about twisting his off like the wishbone on a Christmas turkey.

I couldn't sing worth a damn, but when there were open auditions for a musical in this little college town, and he laughed at the idea, I decided I could wail a few notes as well as the next person. They slammed my ass in the chorus, of course, which was fine with me. I used the opportunity to cut practice and do anything else that would allow me some time alone.

Then came the magic day when I decided that if I was going to be the breadwinner, I would have some fun doing it. My college major was nursing. Not too many jobs out there for someone who *would've* graduated if she could've refrained from making every patient's illness into such a Puccini tragedy that she couldn't stop crying long enough to finish her senior year. So I did what any desperate, hungry, self-respecting young woman would do. I lied. I answered a radio station ad and said with a sweet smile that, yes sir, I could write copy, the best copy you ever saw. The Southern Gentleman thought *this* was such a ridiculous idea that he selflessly took an entire weekend from drankin'-'n'-thankin' with his buddies to spell out for the little woman how the hours would keep me away from the homestead and interfere with my cooking and cleaning, not to mention the stuck-up men I might meet and the opportunities for advancement it might present while I was fifteen whole minutes away from the trailer on Saturdays. And I knew I had hit pay dirt.

Radio was the best time I ever had. I just couldn't believe that they were *paying* me to write copy that I would hear read on the air, and that eventually I would go on the air and play with the equipment myself. Never mind that my first raise was to minimum wage, and that the manager of this little 1,000 watt-er would hand out the last paycheck before Christmas with a great flourish and a hearty "Happy Holidays!" while the check contained not a penny more than the $75 I'd cheerfully busted my butt for. And the day the Southern Gentleman pulled the radio tuner out of the glove compartment of the truck and showed me that it was set on a country station because he absolutely never listened to me on the air, *I knew I was good!!*

But you want to know what the absolute last straw was? When I came home one day with the happy news that I was going to be a mommy, and I went on and on about how wonderful it was going to be for us to share this experience and for him to be present at the delivery of his child (I know, don't throw up), he fed me the line that cut the connection. He said, "That's woman's work."

Those words still bouncing around in my head three months later, I was outta there. And I was blessed with the most wonderful child, my son John, whom I love so dearly. John and I spent the next eight years on our own, before I remarried. We always have been buddies. He's a man now, kind and classy and full of life, with my love of music and the talent to put it into practice on the guitar. We share mutual respect and a special relationship that will last all our lives. I had made the decision to keep only *one* baby—the one I was carrying. It was the smartest decision I ever made.

Wising up is a good thing no matter when it happens. I would not have married this clown if I had realized that I had options. And I bet most of us would have taken a different turn in the road, here and there, if only we had known that there were choices available to us. So I try not to be too hard on people—especially kids—who make similar mistakes. I try to show them they have choices and help them figure out what they are, rather than just tell them. God forbid somebody should do what they think I advised, instead of what they were going to do, and it should go down the tubes. I see now that I should've just told my parents I was grabbing a backpack and heading for Canada or Europe for a little while, or perhaps I should have gone to stay with my wacky and wonderful aunt who lived in Hawaii. (Another rebel. She went there on vacation, about 1940, and liked it so well she never went back to the mainland for any real length of time except for visits. She was there when Pearl Harbor was bombed, and was the giggly little woman who was sunbathing that Sunday morning and waving at a Japanese aircraft as it flew overhead, thinking it was an American who had painted on a "rising sun" just for the hell of it). The brief freak-out my parents might have experienced through my taking time to take stock on a long trip would have been nothing compared to my years of freaking out with "Mr. Achievement."

I don't spend a lot of time thinking about this, and really don't blame anything on anybody, because that takes too much out of **you**. But I do allow myself the occasional secret smile at having advanced so far beyond all of it. The one good thing he did do was to buy a .357 Ruger (only sissies carry smaller weapons, you know), with which I learned to shoot up the Colorado countryside. Women, listen carefully: Target shooting is rewarding in an almost mystical way. First of all, when you have your hand wrapped around a gun, you've got total control over something that's ready to go off whenever you want it to, with absolutely no strings attached. Also, as you try to improve you get immediate results. And it allows you to borrow testosterone-generated terms like shoot, blast, and hammer, and then brag about how well you did. Improving your ability to defend yourself is almost secondary. The last time I went to the firing range I came across a target with a picture of a bad guy who looked so much like the Southern Gentleman, you would have sworn he had posed for it. In the next half hour, I drilled 100 rounds into the area he boasted was home to the "family jewels" (which, since the target was true-to-life, was hard to hit because it was so much smaller than the brain). It was a good range session.

There is a protective-aggressive component to every woman. I call it her "Lioness Chip." Each of us manifests it in her own way and in her own time.

Mine seems to have hijacked a good portion of my brain at an early age. Perhaps it had something to do with my military upbringing. During my father's decades in the army, we did a lot of moving and traveling—New Jersey, Germany, Italy, Virginia, Albuquerque, Denver, Albuquerque . . . I had no idea what it was like to have the same classmates for more than a year or two at a time, and because it's a way of life that all military kids share to this day, none of us thought anything about it. We said hello, we said good-bye. The one important thing to remember was that if you loaned something to somebody, you'd better get it back before the family shipped out and your beloved skate key or dress-up doll (or in my case, my favorite fake pearl-handled Annie Oakley six-shooter) became only a fond memory. The really good thing about growing up in the military is that you become a very adaptable person. You are used to traveling light with a toy collection that's constantly ridded of extraneous or duplicate items, and you know your family will not amass a houseful of pets, because it's that much harder to move when the time inevitably comes.

You also learn to take the concept of military preparedness to heart, even in the playground. I remember in the second grade—on an army base during recess—a nasty little bully approached me menacingly, demanding I relinquish the basketball, threatening me with unspeakable humiliation because his father outranked mine. I gave him the ball, all right, squarely on the forehead. That, I felt, was justified. I admit certain other incidents were clear illustrations of the need for tempering my behavior. For example much earlier, during those wild preschool days in southern Germany, there was the affair involving my little friends who were busy neatening the autumn garden, raking fallen leaves into little *in-order* Teutonic piles. Now, I have nothing against the Germans. I visit the country every chance I get, have very dear German friends, and, in fact, am half German, myself—my father's side, the quiet ones who think before they speak and never become involved in family arguments with members of the other side, the Italians. Italians, as you know, will argue about anything, especially in the kitchen. Among them, cooking is very dangerous with more than one member of the same family in the kitchen at the same time, and especially if any of them have access to anything sharp. I have witnessed discussions over the preparation of tomato sauce that ended with wishes of slow and painful death, and curses upon the genitalia of generations of innocent, unborn descendants.

Even the way my parents met and became engaged was a textbook example of Italian tenacity and German reason. It was a hot, New Jersey, June day during World War II. Mother, Carmen Evangelista, who lived near Newark, heard that there was a cute sergeant in the army recruiting office there, and she set about finding a way to meet him and engage him in conversation—and engage him, period. She went into his office and liked what she saw: John Russell, a large, blond man with kind green eyes, a sense of humor that never rested, and a steady manner that put you completely at ease. So she feigned interest in joining the army. If you knew her, you'd know that Mother is anything but a follower; her tenure would've lasted two weeks before they kicked her out for refusing to button her blouse the way everybody else did, or trying to improve the mess hall kitchen on spaghetti day. Daddy still says he married her to keep her out of the slammer.

He dissuaded her from pursuing a career in the service, but she would not be turned away from her real goal. She virtually lay in wait for him for days and days at the bus stop just outside, a picture of perfection in defiance of the summer humidity that was wilting everything around her. She was perfectly groomed, all five-foot-two of her. Her long, shiny dark hair was neatly pulled back into a low bun, her summer dress was without a crease, and her high heels were impeccably white. She spent hours and hours standing there, pretending over and over that she had missed her bus, until he materialized and they ran into each other again. She took him home to Mama and Papa, fed him, and charmed him. He met most of her six brothers and sisters. The whole scene made sense to a North Dakota boy well into his thirties, with eight siblings of his own and a yen to settle down. He never knew what hit him. She chased him till he caught her.

But back to the German leaf-raking undertaking when I was a little girl. My Italian half felt very strongly that little was to be gained through what it considered pathologically perfect horticultural conduct. After all, one visit to Rome will leave you with the indelible impression that Roman schools take points off for neatness, in a country that still has not straightened up 2,000-year-old fallen columns lying in complete disarray in the middle of its largest city. So, my German playmates, unaware of the enemy in their midst, were taken completely by surprise when I strongly objected to their correcting the way I was tossing the leaves, like a salad, into heaps with interesting shapes. Was Bernini corrected? Was Michelangelo? I took issue. They conferred. My little friend Claus told me that his way was the way it always had been done. I told him, in my best seven-year-old Sophia Loren one-hip-out, one-hand-up posture, that was not the way I always had done it. They conferred again, this cadre of sweet, blond second graders, perhaps discussing only at whose house they would have ice cream, later. But my DNA had begun talking to itself, assessing similar confrontations on German turf. Their orderly, quiet conferencing took on sinister implications. In an effort to roll my tanks first, I hoisted my broom and smacked Claus several times upside the head with it, nearly creating an international crisis between American guest families and their German hosts. As you can see, learning the value of physical restraint would have been a good thing, there. (It occurs to me that Claus appeared so totally bewildered that I now believe that incident may have been my earliest encounter with the whole male-female miscommunication thing. To this day, he probably has no idea why I hit him.)

Later, as a teenager, when I found myself sitting one night in a car beside a Neanderthal with twelve hands and boundless energy, I came to understand the more serious benefits of the

kind of disciplined self-defense that martial arts can provide—
the concept of your body as the only weapon that someone
can't take away from you *and use against you.* It is a talent that
comes in especially handy during those unsettling blind-date
moments, and those sporadic slap-fights in the express line at
the A&P the evening before Rosh Hashanah.

Quite often, even the *suggestion* of a woman's ability to hit
a guy so hard that when he stops rolling his clothes will be out
of style is all you need to improve your day. On a recent hot,
spring afternoon, I went into a liquor store for cognac (for
cooking, I swear) and I stepped up to the register, breaking
through a circle of a half-dozen burly, sweaty beer and wine
delivery men who were in no mood to move. I was wearing
short sleeves, which revealed the tattoos I'd gotten to celebrate
my two black belts, which I'll tell you more about in a minute.
When the startled, Korean clerk recognized the words *pil sung,*
"Certain Victory," emblazoned on my arm and asked me
about them, I explained my bone-crunching training, with special emphasis on the incredibly painful and incapacitating effects of breaking one's legs and the ease with which that can
be accomplished regardless of the opponent's size. The six mus-
cular delivery men *took two steps backward in unison.* It was
like a water ballet, and I was Esther Williams, in the middle!
Repeating my request for them to make room eventually probably would have worked, but this was so much more entertaining. And maybe one of them had a daughter who now is
studying a martial art because Dad saw the quiet confidence it
can give a woman for all of her life.

I happen to be devoted to Choi Kwang Do, because I've

always thought it was "strong enough for a man, but made for a woman" with all those great natural, powerful, *circular* movements that do what they set out to do and then set you up for the next move almost effortlessly. Learning those moves, that punching and kicking, also has the oddest effect on the way a woman interacts with male friends, out in public. Picture this: One day I was sitting with a male acquaintance at the bar of the classy Cafe Intermezzo on the north side of Atlanta, run by my Bundesblonde friend, Renate, with the aforementioned German efficiency I have grown to admire, after all. One of his friends joined us, and they engaged in some typical male bantering about their past sports exploits, body building, victories, and defeats—the sorts of things boys of all ages talk about, and girls of all ages enjoy hearing. As the conversation became more animated and the voices grew louder, a stranger on the other side of me mumbled a disparaging remark to the effect that when I was ready to talk to a *real* man, he'd be there. I blew it off, but they demanded to know what he had said. When I told them, the subject shifted to which of them could mess him up the worst. The boys actually were arguing, in this quiet little place, over who would get to whip his butt. I expected that at any moment one of them would jump up and yell, "Da Bears!" My money was on the fearless, enormous one who had played professional hockey and still had wet dreams about fighting on the ice. Any more testosterone in that room, and I was going to have to open a window. Finally it ended when I realized that I felt very left out—that *I* wanted a shot at him, if one were to be taken. I told them firmly and quietly that if anybody were going to get to take him out it would be me, since I was the person to whom he had spoken. This made sense to them. They stopped. And looked at each other. And agreed that I could do it if I wanted. By that time, the poor sonofabitch had left.

In the past few years I've discovered that this confidence, this well-meaning Xena Warrior Princess–like benevolent, feminine, controlled aggression can also serve you well professionally, if you're willing to put yourself on the line to protect someone who doesn't want to muss up his suit or wreck her manicure to try to fight off the bad guys. It will also be useful for dealing with overly appreciative fans who don't understand that a closing door is not an invitation to a test of strength with the person on the other side.

Bodyguard work is a natural by-product of private investigation. If you're licensed to carry a concealed weapon, which, truly, you hope to God you'll never have to use, and you happen to be proficient in a martial art, and you are well versed in the psychology of handling difficult situations—something you learn during your private investigation education—then you are better prepared than the average person to offer assistance to high-profile individuals who don't want to have to worry about their physical well-being when they're out in public.

There have been a lot of interesting little moments when I have agreed to go along and act as "nanny" to adults, and sometimes children, who don't want to always look over their shoulder. Unfortunately, there's so much I'm not allowed to

reveal about bodyguarding/executive protection. The produc-
ers of the *Tom Snyder Show* wanted me to come on the air to
talk about it and were quite disappointed when I felt I had to
decline to give the specifics of jobs I've worked, and to name
names. Part of the deal, when I agree to protect someone is
that I will safeguard his or her privacy. The very fact that I'm
there for that purpose ought to be strictly confidential. It has
to be, for the job to work well. I'm such a high-profile person
myself, it's better for outsiders to wonder where the big, burly,
thick-necked bodyguards are, when they don't see them. For
instance, I couldn't tell you about the singer who flew to town
with her "exclusive boyfriend," and had arranged to rendez-
vous with her *other* "exclusive boyfriend" in the same hotel.
To keep the peace, keep the noise down, and protect my client
from public embarrassment and possible private battering from
one of those exclusive boyfriends, it was necessary to keep them
separated—even though they were only one floor apart. I did
this without even the hotel knowing what was going on, because people love to talk.

One night in the elevator, all hell broke loose. The singer
and I and boyfriend 1 had just gotten in to ride down to the
lobby, when the elevator stopped and the doors opened on my
worst nightmare: boyfriend 2, who had been into the cooking
wine all afternoon and couldn't even *spell* discretion (I don't
think he could spell it sober). He began with, "Baby where
you been? I ain't seen you all day and you promised me, from
the heart . . ." as his hand found the gold medallion hanging
somewhere near the center of his chest, and his rheumy eyes
wandered from her face to boyfriend 1, who took a half step

toward him like he was going to rearrange him. I couldn't decide whether to stand back or get between them and try to engage the happy couple in loud conversation, hoping boyfriend 2 would be bewildered enough that by the time we got to the lobby the rest of us could make a clean escape. I also could have backed the guy up against the opposite wall of the elevator, take him gently but firmly by his arm or whatever was closest, flash him a big, lascivious smile, bat my lashes, and tell him how good he looked. Given his condition, I went with this option, and it worked. He was stunned and flattered at the attention, and it crossed my mind that I was going to have a bigger problem when I ran into him again somewhere, but that could wait. At the lobby, the singer and I hustled boyfriend 1 out into the crowd, as I yelled over my shoulder to boyfriend 2 that he should stop to check for a big, ugly wet spot on the back of his pants.

This, my friends, was not really brilliant, deductive thinking. It was a scenario I'd considered before, and this whole story is a good lesson about the ways women can take care of themselves. Sure, there was a third option if it had appeared that I ought to decommission him before the other guy did something to him that would have the cops there, but that never happened. And the moral of the story is that it's always better to avoid a messy confrontation than to let one happen and then have to deal with it. And one of the best ways to do that is to prepare yourself by planning what you'd do if you were, for instance, alone in an elevator with someone who became a threat. Or plan what you'd do if someone tried to carjack you in the parking lot of the supermarket. Many, many experts suggest that it's better to take your chances right where you are, because when you get in a car with someone else in charge, you have lost your freedom and your options and you are on the road to disaster. This is a personal choice each of us has to make, and it should be made before such a thing ever happens. Think about it. Think about what you'd do if someone came up to you at the ATM, appeared to be armed, and demanded your cash. I say, give it to them. A *lot* of people, people who love a good fight and have a better than average chance of winning, also agree with me. It's a matter of assessing the situation. The grand master of my martial art, whose name is Kwang Jo Choi, is of slight build but it's all muscle. He was a ninth-degree Tae Kwan Do master when he established the Korean-American street fighting that I have come to love, Choi Kwang Do. (There are days, in traffic here in Atlanta, the Olympic Traffic City from Hell, when I'd almost pay money for some truly threatening creep to reach through the window of my car and grab me, just once.) The difference between this and other martial arts is that the movements are very fluid, much less damaging to the joints, and very applicable to everyday life. Master Choi is benevolent and kind, always smiling, and the only thing that belies his underlying physical genius is the fact that he moves like a cat. He is so good, so fast, so accurate, that he could slice some smart-ass street thug like bacon. But one day, a student asked him, "Master Choi, what would you do if someone came up to you with a knife and demanded your wallet?" And he replied, "I would do this," as he kept a firm eye on his opponent, slowly moving his right hand behind him. He pulled out his wallet and offered it. He explained matter-of-factly, "You could take him on, but somebody's gonna get cut, and what for?"

So allow me to offer these thoughts for you to consider: think ahead. Assess your skills and imagine possible scenarios. Be realistic. And come up with a few game plans that could save your life. No one but you can decide what would be best for you. Apply yourself to this task, take the time to consider this, and refresh your memory periodically.

My Lioness Chip also drove me from investigative and bodyguard work to join the Fulton County (Atlanta) Sheriff's Department as a deputy in the reserve division. For "reserve," read "doesn't get paid." Reserve officers undergo the same training and must meet the same qualifications as regular duty deputies. Most of my training was to prepare me for work as a jail officer at the stark, seven-story palace known among cops as the Fulton County Hilton. It's not true that the gourmet jail food was the biggest reason I joined—a joke, of course, but believe me, the kitchen of this county-run facility produces some seriously satisfying Southern cookin'. The gravy and potatoes are habit-forming.

There's something about helping to keep the peace that I like, along with the comraderie that goes with it, among officers of the law. I'm on leave now, and I miss the deputies with whom I worked, all of whom brought me into the fold and appreciated our joint efforts. I also miss the opportunity to direct traffic and explain to tourists on crowded street corners during the annual black student spring funfest known as "Freaknik" how to walk to the wedding of their niece at the Marriott without feeling obligated to buy marijuana or something stronger from total strangers who have parked their cars in the middle of the street. They effectively shut down the heart of the city for three days, playing their radios so loud that the bass is causing the windows of buildings to move with the beat.

And as a female deputy sheriff I was called upon to search females for LSD and such fun substances outside the Grateful Dead concerts. On one occasion I had to ask a school teacher in tie-dyes and Nikes (yeah, those schoolteachers want you to *think* they're innocent) to reach under her shirt and undo her bra to see what might, uh, fall out. When this tricky little clothing maneuver was over, we knew each other better than we wanted to. I didn't find anything, not even an attractive psychedelic licking stamp. It was at that point that the teacher recognized me . . . and her scream echoed through the parking decks: "My God! I've just been searched by *Lynne Russell!!*" More than one passing Dead fan appeared ready to get in line for that, and it occurred to me that night, as I unstrapped my body armor and got ready for bed, that if times ever got hard, if I ever returned from vacation to find my company had changed the entry passcode on me while I was gone—don't laugh, such industry jokes are based in truth—I could always put on my uniform and sell tickets for body searches.

———

Doesn't it just make you crazy when you hear women referred to as a segment of the population unable to make it without special help? Since when? Over the centuries, who *else* has assumed responsibility for pregnancy? Delivering a child? Delivering "size doesn't matter" in a way that sounds convincing? Breast-feeding? Waxing? Five extra pounds of water a month? Learning to navigate in high heels without listing, as you go around corners? We do owe special thanks to a man for inventing the brassiere, although it has been rumored that he had an ulterior motive.

We don't need special favors because our plumbing is the way it is. We just need the same rules and the same opportunities. And the same American Express card. And we need to learn six very important things. The first one is something that little boys seem to grow up already knowing. Something at which we must become adept, especially until we are the happy recipients of the aforementioned perks:

1. ***Make Your Own Odds.*** I learned this quite by accident. I was living in Honolulu and working at a local TV station, anchoring and reporting . . . grueling days of working the military beat, which involved endless mornings on a boat in Kanaohe Bay watching young, healthy marines do rappelling exercises out of speedboats, with the golden Hawaiian sun and gentle trade winds lulling me into a near-coma. The most worrisome part was being awake in time to get back to the station and edit the tape. (Oh hell, I'm not in church, but I'm going to confess something to you anyway:

my station still was making money the old-fashioned way . . . by shooting news footage on *film*. Actually, it was quite expensive, but the new, state-of-the-art cameras were more expensive. So, while the rest of the world had gone to videotape, we were shooting stories—sparingly—on film. We had to get back in time to edit the stuff, sure, but first to develop it.)

One day, in the midst of news stories on lei-making contests and orchid shows, the proverbial "hard news" struck. Philippines leader Ferdinand Marcos was to visit Hawaii and say some important things at a huge gathering at a country club, and I was to cover it. The giggle-of-the-day was that Hawaii businessmen of all professions are accustomed to wearing colorful, floral "Aloha shirts" every day of the week, and the Secret Service, charged with providing security during the Marcos visit, knew this. In an effort to blend in, the agents showed up in shirts with palm trees and piña coladas on them, a whole cadre of guys in bright colors and sunglasses, with wires coming out of their ears. As it happened, on that particular day the guests at the luncheon decided to wear conservative suits. And the Secret Service could not have been more conspicuous.

After the speech, as Marcos moved toward his limousine through the throng of reporters and bystanders, I wanted to catch him to ask him some questions. So as the crowd jostled me and my photographer, I yelled to the nearest Secret Service agent, "What are the odds

I can get him to stop long enough to talk?" The agent shouted back, *"Make your own odds, Lynne!"*

His words ring in my ears to this day. I wish I could find him and thank him, maybe give him a little tour of CNN and treat him to a signed photo of Bobbie Battista. He had no way of knowing that his words would be passed from me to thousands and thousands of women across America women who have told me years later that making their own odds changed their lives. I have received letters from women as far away as Japan, thanking me for the words of encouragement that somehow reached them and played a part in improving their lives, empowering their present, and enriching their future.

Make the game yours. Change the rules, if you have to. Once you have altered the equation and you have a greater chance of winning what you are after, you will find you have everything it takes to go for it and get it.

2. ***Listen to Advice.*** It's free, and Lord knows there's enough of it. Some of it might even help. One of the most attention-getting advice phrases came my way when I was listening to my friend, Linda, trying to talk someone out of jumping headlong into a relationship. She was reminded that he had been divorced only a month. Perhaps you will agree with other dating women that until a man *you don't know* has been turned loose at least six months, most of what he says and does with you has more to do with the woman he just left than with you. And, though she did not

ask to see a financial statement, it was not a good omen that on their first date his credit card was declined when he picked up their theater tickets. And he always seemed preoccupied. Because of that and a few other things, our infatuated friend spent sleepless nights pondering and agonizing over what the hell she was doing wrong with him—on those occasions when he was so detached from her that he acted like his brain had been sucked out of his head. It certainly appeared that this was not the best horse to bet on, but she wouldn't listen. Then Linda put it into language we all could understand: "This situation has so many flashing red lights, you need sunglasses." Somehow that got her attention and put her to thinking. *And that's all advice has to do for you to benefit from it—it just gets you working it out in your head.* So listen, and don't interrupt. The people who know you best may have insight that you just aren't capable of developing on your own, because you're too close to the situation.

3. *Any Reason Is a Good Reason If It's Yours.* You look back on the things you've done and you're amazed at how stupid you really were. Could this be the same person as the sophisticated woman-of-the-world who stares back at you now from the mirror? Yes, it could. You've done things knowing perfectly well you were placing yourself in the Fools Hall of Fame. Consider this scenario: an intelligent woman, mother of two daughters, and Keeper of the Flame at an office that would fall apart without her, married the same guy

twice. Not because it was such a good idea, but because "We were downtown, it was April 15, and I had just filed taxes and I was in a rotten mood anyway, so I thought what the hell, why not." She knew better, she really did. She was just tired of fighting the good fight, with the two kids and a first husband who didn't like to pay child support. Her reason was that she was just plain exhausted and needed a break. The second round with this guy lasted longer than it should have, but just long enough for her to see that it was time to blow a hole in the wall and make a break for it. The point is, when you do what you have to do, don't beat yourself over the head for it later. You did it, you had your reasons, and now you're going to fix it, that's all. There are plenty of people in this world who are standing in line to tell you what you *should* have done. Screw 'em. You've already figured that out. It's like going to a psychic and being totally amazed that she's telling you so much about your recent past. What the hell good is that, I already know it. Give me something on the future if you really want to help.

4. ***Be Realistic.*** Understand that certain things are just facts of life, especially when they pertain to women and men. You can call them Universal Truths. Like, women get cellulite and men get muscle. Another one, a truth that transcends societies, economic strata, and vast bodies of water, relates to a woman's *realistic* expectations from a relationship with a man. It comes from an astute woman in the upper echelons of Turner

Broadcasting management—a Georgia girl whose soft, Southern drawl masks a brain so sharp they call it the Internet Browser. Here it is: It doesn't matter how wonderful a man is, if you clutch him to your bosom because you're attracted to him, you'll find him all warm and cuddly, like a puppy. But if you take that puppy home with you he *will* wind up peeing on your carpet. In other words, relationships get deep and they get messy. They just do. And when that happens, it's often the woman who has to do the cleaning up, since she so often gives too much of herself. And she does it over and over, until one day she finds herself condensing all the philosophy of the puppy story into a four-word message to the opposite sex: "Fuck *all* uh y'all!" Her expectations were unrealistic.

5. *Extreme Measures.* Sometimes you have to take them, to get the job done. You'll like this one, there's a lot of humor to it. A frustrated news colleague, an attractive, assertive-but-gracious woman of journalistic experience and good common sense, possesses a commendable tolerance for office politics. She also has a potentially lethal intellect, reined in by diplomacy and good taste. I was surprised when she marched into the closet I call an office and wanted to brainstorm about the daily meetings she had just begun attending, as the only woman in a room full of men in suits. She felt the results of the most recent meeting were disturbingly inadequate, because nobody would listen to what she was trying to say. She was the only one at the

conference table with the sort of plumbing that results in a voice just high enough to be ignored when all the baritones begin booming at each other over one issue or another. If she had been offering cold beer and chips during a commercial break, she might have had everyone's attention. She felt this situation was threatening to affect some important decisions, and she wanted to talk about how to make her own odds, how to be taken seriously. This surprised me, as I always saw her as a force with which to be reckoned. I was sure that if she ever unleashed that fire, the whole place would get singed. She suggested to me that she was just on the verge of marching into the next meeting and plunking a huge, plastic version of the Male Masterpiece on the conference table in front of her and saying, "Okay, gentlemen, now we *all* have one. Can we get please get down to business?" This would give new meaning to the term demonstration tool.

We agreed that another approach might work just as well. Anything but soft-spoken and shy, I always have found it beneficial to be able to outshout men at a voice level that is within their auditory range, the lower the better. Of course it's best not to have to resort to bellowing an obscenity to secure a lull in the conversation, but that is a battle tactic not to be ignored. As they look at you in astonishment, you have an opening for making a statement. Be advised, though, that this will work only twice in a row, and only intermittently thereafter, so it should be employed sparingly.

On another front, this colleague had tried wearing female versions of the male suit, but she did not feel comfortable in them, and all they did was turn her into Pee-wee Herman with longer hair. It didn't work to try to become more like a man, and why should she? She didn't see any of the men wearing perfume or earrings in order to bond with *her*. She decided to be nothing but her extremely feminine self. If that affected the equilibrium of a few of the gentlemen in the room, well, it's an imperfect world. So she began to wear the clothes she loved, modified for business and for effect: a straight leather skirt, yes, but a long one because, as all good dressers will tell you, you should accentuate the positive, which for her happened to be above the waist.

6. ***Clothing Corollary.*** I found out quite the hard way over the years, an important lesson about wardrobe, and it has as much to do with your image as a woman who takes charge of her life, as anything else. I have spent thousands and thousands of dollars on the purchase and maintenance of lovely clothes I never would have owned, had I not had to maintain a certain level of well-groomed, refreshed appearance on the air. And on many occasions, I have found myself with a dilemma: what to wear for a special appearance or a special night on the air or a special photo shoot. There

have been times when I have opted for an outfit solely because someone else liked it or because I had spent so damn much money on it I was not going to let it sit in the closet. I can thank another colleague, Lori, a hard-working young woman packing for her first anchor job in California, for reminding me of my own cardinal wardrobe rule. She called me for advice on whether she should wear lime green for a billboard photo. I asked her if she looked good in that color, and she was very enthusiastic, about it, but she wasn't sure whether she should wear it. I worked on all the aspects of that, and then was embarrassed that I had not remembered my own best piece of advice: *If you look fabulous in it, wear it. If you don't, don't even have it in the closet.*

On the air and off, you cannot afford to look "marginal" a single day in your life. Why should you? Talk about making your own odds. This is so important, and it begins before you even leave the house! It's better to wear a basic wardrobe of neutrals (black, beige, white, shades of brown) with an occasional splash of color, in assorted, soft textures that make you feel like a million, than to wear a different $1,000 suit every day that looks only average on you.

And by the way, forget all that "Color Me This" and "Color Me That, Under White Light" nonsense. Georgette Mossbacher, former head of a huge cosmetics empire, and a gorgeous redhead, delights in wearing the color red and looking fabulous in it. This flies in the face of all the geniuses who preach against it as they point to graphs and and color charts and mumble theories from "experts." If you like a color, if you really, really feel you come alive in it and it flips a switch in the part of you that sends out good vibrations and makes you want to call Donald Trump for a date, then wear it! *You* are the first person you have to please when you look in the mirror. And whatever your job is, you'll do it better when you feel fabulous. Don't stop till you can say "*Damn*, I look good" on the way out of the house.

It's My Party and I'll Do What I Damn Well Please

L ife is too short not to live it the way you want to. It isn't a matter of money. It's attitude. It's giving up old limitations and understanding you have choices. Begin by believing that everything is possible.

For example, I recently relocated to a new place in the center of town. A fresh beginning and a new opportunity to shake off old preconceptions about how a house should be run; to make my own rules, and to furnish and live in it in a completely different way.

I began by seeing quite clearly, as I walked into the wonderful, empty space so full of promise and possibilities, that it doesn't matter at all what people think of the way you live. You're the one spending your days and nights in your own home, so why arrange it contrary to what is the most comfortable for you? If your friends don't understand what you're doing, just smile sweetly and remind them that you're sure they want you to be happy, and this way *you are*. Sure, you can make some adjustments to accommodate your friends: I had put the piano in what was meant to be the dining room, which left no place for them to put down a plate at dinnertime. So I finally capitulated and put in a little table for meals. I got the one I fell in love with, which happens to be so small that if four people share it, they are very well acquainted by the end of dinner because they've been rubbing knees all night. But that's fine; when I dine by myself I somehow always wind up sitting on the floor or on the couch in front of a quaint, also little, antique table.

I think that in another life I must have been a bedouin or an Indian, someone who lived in a tent. I just love sitting on the floor to do everything from eating dinner to writing monthly checks, and I always have been very happy with my mattress on the floor. It came to me as I was daydreaming in an elevator the other day, that from the time of my first marriage as a teenager until only recently, when I came across a bed frame I just had to have, I've slept on the floor. This seems perfectly natural to me. It gives a whole new meaning to "rolling out of bed." On days when it's excruciatingly hard to get up, you don't have to. You can crawl to the bathroom, following the trail of clothes you left the night before, and pull yourself up slowly to sneak up on your bleary-eyed image in the bathroom mirror. Though you may miss the bouncy effect you can achieve with a box spring, you literally are able to "fall into bed" at night without worrying about missing your mark and doing any permanent damage. Best of all, with the walls draped in a warm-looking, pale silk and a huge, fringey lampshade hanging from the ceiling, the effect is quite cozy and charming—to the extent that the maintenance men in my building won't tell me how to lift the hair trap out of the shower to clean it, because they look forward to walking through the bedroom to do it themselves.

And I have banished gymnasium lighting from my house. There is enough harshness elsewhere in this world. When I come home, I want to be soothed, to have my own place wrap itself around me, welcome me back, relax me immediately. So all my lights are on dimmer switches, and you won't find a bare bulb anywhere. Except for a couple of good reading lamps, all the lights are a soft pink or amber. The effect is fabulous. Only one person ever has commented, "You don't like light much, do you?" But I forgive him, because whatever he says, he enjoys being here because I'm here. And there's plenty of natural light from the windows during the day, mostly filtered through very sheer fabric to soften it.

All the other elements of my place lend themselves to this mellow lighting approach. When I was living with someone else, I went through the matching draperies, matching furniture, matching everything phase. And the two futons, one Japanese screen and a low butcher-block-living-room-table, minimalist phase. I was sure all my friends thought these were the product of very advanced thinking. I know I impressed the hell out of myself. Even then, soft indirect lighting felt best. But when I let myself go and did what I wanted without thinking about anybody else's ideas, I created a sensuous little haven. It's very eclectic, furnished with things that appeal to me and feed my soul; somehow it all seems to come together. As I look around I actually smile when I see the crystal chandeliers and old lampshades—or old-*looking* lampshades that I've dipped in a strong espresso mixture to make them look as if they were dragged out of a Berlin house of the night, just before the war. I love the framed etchings of Paris and the mirrors everywhere, mostly with little lamps reflected in them to create twice the effect and twice the light. There's a bronze of Winged Victory, a delicate, alabaster madonna, a charming Bacchus with his grapes. There are always lots of candles, one of them borne high by a foot-and-a-half-tall bronze cupid who looks as if he's about to fly off the little couch table. The antique Italian inlaid chest is accompanied by prints from the Louvre, overlapping carpets, and so much fringe and velvet and sensuous texture, it looks like an explosion in a bordello. Many of these things, the little things easy to carry on a plane or check through as baggage, I've brought back from Europe, so that along with rendering immediate pleasure each time I am near them, they remind me of happy times in France or Berlin.

The things you have around you, whatever they are, must do the same for you. If you're ambivalent about anything you're living with, make it a priority to fix that—get rid of it or change it in some way—as soon as you can. True, most of the time it isn't possible to rush out and do a complete change of your furnishings, because it's way too expensive. And that's kind of good, because the process is half the fun; and it actually takes time to create and develop the surroundings that make you most comfortable. You have to do it by feel, a little here and a little there. Speaking of feel, when you're in a store and you see something that appeals to you, close your eyes and touch it. Does the sensory part do anything for you? If it's a little pillow or a piece of fabric or a chenille throw, how does it *feel?* If it looks good but it doesn't feel fabulous, don't waste your money on it. Be picky about what you bring into your home. Insist that everything *be satisfying to the touch.* Anything less, and you're shortchanging yourself. Get used to this new approach, and you'll never go back to the old way.

There are other adjustments you'll want to make to the place you call home. This one doesn't cost a dime. My philosophy about housework is that if you get it dirty you have to clean it. So if using something doesn't make you absolutely crazed with joy, don't even touch it. The stove, for instance. The first thing I did on the first day in my new place was to walk over to the breaker box and turn off the stove. Now the oven is home to fax paper and printer paper; and I keep a word processor on top of the stove, together with lovely bottles of wine and my favorite bust of Beethoven planted elegantly to the side. It works for me. The microwave still is there, so no one starves waiting for the champagne to be opened. But once again, there is the occasional adjustment to be made, on behalf of someone worth caring about—like a man who loves to cook, and who leaves the kitchen looking as if no one had been there. For him, the stove gets turned on, although it's hell remembering to take the paper out of the oven. On one particular nice, romantic Saturday night of *al dente* pasta and luscious, fragrant tomato sauce, the word processor did experience near meltdown, but it was an event to remember. Like everything else in life, go with your best judgment; remember that when it comes to those few square feet that you can control, you can change the rules as you go.

It's okay that I have a little cache of instruction booklets filed in the kitchen cabinet where the tomato sauce and soup ought to be. It's another symbol of freedom from convention; and it's an indicator of my disdain for the obligation and new sense of responsibility we all feel whenever we spend our hard-earned money on a technological product that we'll never understand. A product that will blink and flash at us until we want to smash it. My theory on technology is simple: Use it or it will GET you! Who among us hasn't sworn that if one more thing beeps at us, we're going to go postal? Nothing wrong with feeling that way, there's a reason for it. We don't realize how much of ourselves we are giving up to all the devices that were designed to *make our lives easier.* They really have made life infinitely more complicated, because they require care, batteries, plugs, and *education.*

Admit it, you own at least one piece of advanced machinery that you've spent good money for, that you don't know how to operate to its full potential, because you're so busy earning money to buy those things, you haven't had the time to figure out how to make them work. I have a stack of manuals on electronic products that I'll read one day before the damn things break. Meanwhile, I could feel guilty every day that I don't do it, had I not devised a way out, and here it is: Give yourself a break—cut yourself some slack—and realize that it isn't fair to punish yourself for not doing it all perfectly. Pick up *one* manual and allow *one* day to hit the highlights. Find, in the contents, the things that are important to you and target them. You may find that since you bought the product you don't care about a single thing in the manual, that you've lost interest; that's okay because now it's off your back. The manual you pick up may be the one you think will be the easiest, but I'm betting you're going to go for the instructions on the most expensive thing you bought, because you're *still* pissed that you spent $500 for a purse-size electronic personal organizer/word processor that spell-checks, faxes, files, cross-references, downloads, uploads, and calls your mother, but all you know how to do with it is look up addresses. Enough already. Don't be ashamed to admit it was a bad purchase, a waste of money. Because now you move to what the world loves to call "the healing process": you're going to decide that you'll *never* use it for anything other than addresses because *you choose not to*, and that will be that. In fact, even as I write this, I am packing the damn thing in its original box with all three untouched instruction books (three, can you believe it?) and am preparing to sell it to a college student for fifty bucks. Since there have been days when I would have *paid* fifty bucks to get it out of my sight, I consider this a healthy move.

"Living it your way" does mean amassing a wealth of information that does not come out of instruction books. Things you always wanted to know in areas that will benefit you on a daily basis, and things that will make absolutely no difference whatsoever in the way you run your life. You just want the fun of picking up the facts. The very knowledge of the effort that it took to fit it into your busy life, the feeling of achievement, will stay with you and enhance your confidence. Keep learning. The rush you get just signing up for the classes is worth it.

Sometimes you need a kick in the ass to do it, but then you're grateful later. Case in point: I know a man who is a veritable smorgasbord of extracurricular achievement, and for a while he delusionally thought I was, too. How to keep up such an image, when someone is displaying boundless enthusiasm and is expecting you to come up with something new, too? He is a successful businessman, a former professional athlete, a gourmet cook, a woodsman; he spends a lot of time weight training, he has a boat captain's license, he is a certified expert SCUBA diver. This last one was the broadside kick. I'd always wanted to dive and when he discovered that, he issued me a challenge to learn to do it. Before I knew it, he had provided me with a certification course and advice, right down to insisting on a one-piece swimsuit instead of the two-piecer that tends to be way too much fun. Ignoring my friends' admonitions that if humans were meant to breathe underwater we'd have gills, I agreed to go for it. I did have some reservations, since there was a lot of physics to learn and I never was very good with calculations (to this day, when I balance my checkbook I take the best two out of three answers *with a calculator*), but I decided I didn't want to look back one day and wish I'd done it.

The book learning came first, and I worked to finish it before the first "water day." I decided to make it fun, and sat all Easter afternoon at an outdoor cafe, studying until I lost the light . . . and finished! I was exhausted but exhilarated. It reminded me of when I was a kid and I finished a big homework project on time. It wasn't that often, so it's easy to remember. I really felt good about myself, and when I got up to leave the cafe, I did that superior little walk that Dana Carvey perfected for the Church Lady. I felt I'd earned it. That's the feeling you need to get, not once but repeatedly, all your life. My father always said that when you stop growing you start dying.

Incidentally, for the record and in case you ever are tempted to take up SCUBA diving, I'd like to share an enlightening little discovery. I was told, by my friend whose assessment I believed to be the gospel truth, that when you are diving the air you exhale in cute little bubbles in that beautiful underwater world—where the fishes happily dance around you like those air-headed little birds in Snow White—sounds like lovely music. Well, guess what. My certification dives took place in choppy, open salt water of 63 degrees with 3-foot murky visibility at a depth of 60 feet. Still nauseous from the boat ride out, my eyes filled with disbelief as I stared into the mask of my saucer-eyed "dive buddy" who also by that time had peed his pants. I discovered—and I only wish someone had told me in advance so that it wouldn't have been such a shock—that new divers exhale huge bubbles because *they are scared shitless*, and the sound you hear is not music, but your life's breath escaping your body to join other, more reasonable gaseous molecules, which are *above* water where they are supposed to be, and where you should be, instead of freaking out innocent sea creatures. I just wanted you to know.

I Feel for You, But I Can't Reach You

Let's talk about other people's problems with what you're doing. *It's THEIR problem.* Or as they say in my mother's home state of West Virginia, I feel for you but I can't reach you—I *want* to care that you're distressed about something I'm doing, honey, but I'm not going to waste my time on it because you just don't get it. The sad truth is that you can get away with doing almost any stupid off-the-wall thing, as long as you're under thirty—or a Hollywood star—or a football player—or richer than God. Otherwise, you're elbowing your way through a crowded group of adults who, like yourself, in order to buck the system, must exert the usual effort toward achieving their goals, *plus* extra effort defending themselves. They are defending themselves before slackers who simply blow them off because they find criticizing achievers more rewarding than accomplishing something on their own. That's okay. You can take the time to fight them off, or you can adopt the philosophy of my psychic-extraordinaire friend, Gary Spivey: To hell with 'em. And Gary is a man who needs to think this way. He lived for a while not far from me, here in Atlanta, and I know him well enough to tell you that he is cut from different cloth. If you have seen him in a guest appearance on television or in a national publication, you already know that Gary has a unique presentation. He is the only white boy with an afro. And this afro is sprayed pure white, which gives the effect of a halo framing his round, friendly face. It also gives the effect of an interplanetary visitor, especially this deep into the South, in Newt Gingrich/soccer mom/Civil War "Forget, Hell" territory. In other words, he's a mold-breaker in a very conservative part of the country. I think the folks would've been a lot less taken aback, as they sat in their neighborhood no-alcoholic-beverages-served-in-*this*-place restaurant wolfing down the fried special of the day, if this had been taking place in some bastion of free-thinking a little further up the coast, or all the way over on the left coast in L.A. or San Francisco. He usually wears a loose cotton white shirt and white slacks, under which white boots—with little, thin, one-inch heels—peek out as he moves quickly around the room. The room quite often is his kitchen, where he delights in preparing enormous, gourmet, buffet-style meals while crowds of friends and admirers wander in and out of the kitchen and the house. Not your usual host, not your usual dinner party. You never know who you'll find there. I went over after I got off the air one night, and there was Bertie Higgins, who wrote and recorded "Key Largo," sitting in his bare feet in the living room singing that very song, which always has given me goose bumps. I was blown away. Another night I found myself sitting on the veranda carrying on a conversation with Gary's huge parrot, Seymour, minutes before one of former Hollywood madam Heidi Fleiss's girls and I exchanged thoughts on the male psyche. While all this was going on, there was Gary, cooking—absolutely white head to toe, an angel in the kitchen—a cuddly, intelligent, lovable, entertaining, care-giving person whose huge home is open at any hour to his friends and to people he doesn't even know. He is a perfect example of someone who really needs not to care what other people think of his appearance and lifestyle.

He could go through life in a Brooks Brothers suit, but it just wouldn't feel right. True, it doesn't hurt to develop an unusual appearance to set yourself apart from the truckload of ordinary-looking psychics around the country, but if this spray-paint routine were difficult for him to endure, he wouldn't do it. And why should he have to look like everyone else, just to please other people? Here is a man who really lives his philosophy, and he is comfortable with that.

My tattoos (and maybe yours) fall into this category. One of them, the smaller one, is on the inside of my left, lower arm. It's a little line drawing of a dragon and the Korean symbols that remind me that if you are as well prepared as you possibly can be, if you do your best and you do not give up, you will succeed. This is pretty heady stuff, because you can apply it to every aspect of your life. Certainly it got me through the most physically demanding experience of my life, the black belt test. Passing such a test is a real milestone for a woman, and ought to get her at least as many points as giving birth. Having experienced both, I see now that while both are pain-ful, the black belt exam is a greater test of discipline, because when push comes to shove, with labor, it isn't possible to change our minds and back out at the last minute. Also, we didn't get ourselves to the test through fifteen minutes of ecstasy.

The exam is long and it's difficult. When you think you have performed every pattern of movements for every level up to black belt, perhaps more than once, you engage in defense drills and attack drills. Then you are required to fight opponents, all-out, striking at the air-filled shields they are holding. Then, when you feel you are ready to collapse, you proceed to the board breaks—stacks of wood through which you must thrust a hand or foot or elbow. At this point you have decided that there's no way you are going to have to come back and do all this again, so *something* is going to break, the boards or you, but something's going to give. And you do it. You do it because you were prepared, you didn't stop, and you did your best. You can see why I placed this on the inside of my arm, where I can see it and think on it whenever I needed the reinforcement in any element of my life—inside the "dojang" where we take our Choi Kwang Do lessons or on the street or at my desk.

A couple of years later, I tested for first-degree black belt in an even more grueling display of what I had learned, and by the grace of God was successful again. By then, I was feeling quite wicked, and decided to place a more elaborate but equally meaningful tattoo on the other arm, this time just below the tricep, where the rest of the world could see it. A lovely thought, and I'm glad I did it, but I keep forgetting it's there. Occasionally I go out in a delicate little dress with spaghetti straps, thinking I look the epitome of femininity, when in reality I've taken on the Xena, Warrior Princess/Biker Chick from Hell persona. Do I care? To tell you the truth, no. I try to remember that if I want to tie a nice little bow around my arm and over the big tattoo on this particular evening, I have the option to do so; but if I forget, and some genius casts a disdainful glance or makes a comment, it doesn't make me self-conscious at all. It makes me give him an "I could whip your ass but I might mess up my hair" look and thank him for reminding me that there are people in this world you just don't need to please, and he's one of them.

Isn't that what Xena would do? She's the fictional counterpart to Hercules on television, in the dark, ancient time of centaurs and slaves. Xena is a rebel, whose fighting skills were born during her early years of fending off marauding warlords. She's not a prissy, little wisp of a thing, and there's nothing delicate about her. She ain't Wonder Woman, that's for sure. Her lipstick is not perfect, in fact it doesn't look as if she even wears any; and she certainly is not a perfect size six or eight. There's some meat on those bones. She wears boots all right, but not the kind you shine; and she dresses in a short, brown, leathery skirted number that gives her a lot of room for backflips during sword fighting. You can see how Xena could appeal to a woman like me, who really adores all-out kicking and punching in a martial art, and dreams of reprising those fencing lessons I had in college with real sword-fighting skills. God knows what I'd do with them in Atlanta, but that's not the point. Wouldn't it just be a kick to know you could stand in that long line at the Macy's white sale and if you really wanted you could start a shoppers' riot—whipping around with a loud shriek and bringing down all the displays of draped blankets and bedspreads with just a few swooshes of your mighty sword?

You undoubtedly will encounter some unwanted opposition and attitude toward your brilliant little schemes. Do not be taken aback. Acquaint yourself well in advance with "The Sour Grapes Blow-Off Scale," a form of rationale that the less adventurous and more boring among us employ. They will refer to the scale often, so get used to it. It runs like this: According to your present age, if you pursue something wild and wonderful (to many people this can mean anything besides ironing or switching cigarette brands), you're:

30s	Irresponsible
40s	In Your Second Childhood
50s	Interesting to Observe at a Distance
60s	Senile
70s	Cute but Not to Be Taken Seriously
80s	A Threat

There are all sorts of reasons we refuse to conform to the dullest segment of society's idea of what we should be doing: nothing. Some of us have always loved trying something new and see no reason to stop just when we're getting good at it. Others are encouraged by friends with a bit of vision. Then there are those of us who have been waiting to cut loose since we were thirteen, and for one reason or another just never got around to it, and now are in the mood to raise some hell. Maybe we married young and had kids. That'll suck the steam right out of your engine, won't it. Or maybe we were scared of our parents. I was—not my mellow dad, who was my co-conspirator in life avoiding confrontations on the home front—but my fiery, unpredictable mother, who allowed no leeway in adhering to the rules and regulations, which is kind of funny, since Daddy was the one in the army.

Do you know, the one day I actually summoned the courage to cut a class in the eleventh grade, I was convinced that Mother somehow would know what I was doing, as she seemed to know everything, and it so psyched me out that I never left the school grounds. I was Richie Cunningham in a skirt. I didn't even have the guts to allow myself a delicious, forbidden taste of that traditional senior year transgression of nodding off during study hall. In a huge room filled with too many students for a single teacher to watch—one of whom I remember (boy *do* I, leather jacket, James Dean with red hair) was a boy who would spend the entire hour leaning on his elbows on the desk and defiantly moving his fingers in creative ways that suggested he was flipping off the teacher as he stared intently at him. I was mesmerized by his daring. Me, I was too chicken even to close my eyes. Yet the kids who did skip class, flunk PE, and drive fast cars did not grow up to rip off 7-Elevens. Some of them, in fact, have been wearing suits for years and paying taxes. It's the others, the quiet ones, who are doing twenty years federal for wire fraud or for bringing marijuana bundles the size of Buicks into the country.

Whatever your reason for choosing to walk a different path in this life—you're a natural-born rebel, or the product of friendly prodding, or a bundle of suppressed teenage energy bursting free at last—it's important to remember that you shouldn't take yourself too seriously. All this is supposed to be *fun*. A good way to keep it light and keep from getting angry with people who think we're strange, is to make a regular thing of making fun of ourselves. Beat them to it—in private, of course. Anything else would just confirm their notion that our ship has left the dock. Here's a wonderful way to amuse yourself: Go over the elements of your life that you take for granted—the way you do little things, your habits at home, the order in which you put on your clothes (a sock and a sock, or a sock and a shoe?), your expression as you put on eyeliner, how you act when you're in an elevator alone, the way you try to adjust your underwear in public—and pretend you're a stranger seeing this for the first time. Some of it is very, *very* funny, very Benny Hill. And if you want to take the concept a bit further, it's also reassuring confirmation that even in the small stuff you are "living it your way" and asserting your individuality, and there's nothing anybody can do about it.

To illustrate and encourage you to do this, I am willing to share something I really don't talk much about because it's so embarrassing. If like me you're used to sleeping on the floor, you have to remember to watch out away from home. On two occasions in hotels I have damn near wound up in the emergency room. The most memorable one was the night I had my hand on the bathroom light switch and leaned around the corner to get a fix on the bed, before I turned out the light and negotiated my way through the darkness. Boat captains use the stars to calculate their position; my mind factored in the LED readout on the clock on the nightstand to the left of the bed. I turned out the bathroom light and did a swan dive into the area that I thought was the middle of the bed. The first half of the maneuver went fine, as I landed on my stomach in the wondrous, cushy softness of the trampoline-like Hilton king-size. But the flip to the back side went awry, as I bounced up and off the edge of bed and came down very hard on the floor, jammed up against the outside wall. As I lay there taking inventory, waiting for the pain to begin shooting through my limbs, I imagined myself calling the front desk for a doctor and having to explain how I had dislocated my shoulder and gotten a concussion. I saw the entire, ill-conceived event in slow motion, *and it was the funniest damn thing I had ever seen in my life.* I was laughing so hard I was crying, because it was right out of the movies. I was lucky. Didn't break anything, didn't see the doctor. Also didn't learn anything, because I did it again three years later and missed the bed entirely. I had a bruise on my right cheek for a week; lucky I didn't smash it.

So much for taking yourself too seriously. I also was reminded that when you venture from your little cocoon where you're doing what you damn well please, to the outside world where some of the rules are different, you're going to have to make some adjustments.

Attitude: The Bubbles Aren't All in the Champagne

Why is it that furniture and wine get more respect the older they get—and people, especially women, get less? Why is it that a woman's age is so much more important than her accomplishments? The number that you are means so little. The entire year I was thirty-one, I thought I was thirty-two. Who cares? I have a friend who celebrates her birthday on January first of every year, just because she likes it like that. But then she can't remember whether she's changing it early or late, since she was born in October. Who cares?

Have you ever looked up "age" in the dictionary? You get the feeling it's like a disease, when "ageless" is defined as "seeming not to show the effects of age." And you recall all those nice folks who thought they were doing you a favor when they told you that you were ageless, lucky you. What I want to know is, what's wrong with "the effects of age," when they are wisdom, sensitivity, pragmatism, the loss of that common baby fat, experience, world-class shopping skills, and an attitude that will allow you to enjoy all of that and take full advantage of everything you have, *if only everybody will leave you the fuck alone?*

What if the reverse were true? Suppose the effects of age really were the dreaded lethargy, lack of enthusiasm, lack of confidence, inability to concentrate, and disinterest in the outside world that some older people exhibit? Doesn't that also describe the first boy you dated in junior high, and more than one guy you've met since then? Those things can come along anytime in life. If you don't want them, work against them but don't assume they are inevitable.

It occurs to me that the only people who make a big thing of *your* chronological age, a meaningless number, are the ones who have racked up a few years and aren't happy with where they are. Or they're terrified that one day they will find themselves in that position . . . and after all, nobody likes to suffer alone. So you get birthday cards with age as the theme—jokes about California redwoods and prairie fires on birthday cakes. When those things come to me, even from well-meaning high-school classmates, I just can't relate to them. I don't get it. And I feel sorry for the people who send them, because they deserve to feel more *alive*.

Someone once quipped, "How old would you be if you didn't know how old you were?" I'd be about twenty-nine or thirty, how about you? Interviewers always want to know how old you are. That always takes me by surprise, since I spend so little time thinking about it, and I hardly ever have remembered to ask anyone *I* was interviewing about that. I'd like to ask why it matters, but then I know I'd become, "Lynne Russell, who declines to give her age." So depending on my mood, I tell them it's all over the Internet, or I just tell them what it is, and suggest that even bothering to mention it does such a disservice to every person, especially women. There's no question that the public tends to categorize us by age, and put us in little boxes labeled "twenty and still young," "thirty and still pretty," "Forty (to paraphrase Joan Rivers) and her body is falling so goddamn fast her gynecologist needs a hard hat," "fifty and a grandmother," "sixty and it's over." I guess the rest of the world isn't going to change its perspective until we do. The less our number means to us, the less it will mean to everyone else. And then, one brilliant day, instead of casting a critical eye as a woman fulfills her destiny, the ones in charge will hand out days off and shopping points on every anniversary of her birth.

My own mother is fond of telling me to "dress my age." I don't know what that means. When she was my age, she was dressing like Richie's mom on *Happy Days*, with that Phyllis Schlafly updo and a shirtwaist dress, and she looked fabulous. It really was her, and it's still her favorite. God bless her. For me, it's the great, black turtleneck catsuit and over-the-knee boots that prompted Ted Turner to interrupt an important news programming meeting to announce, "Ah, I like that outfit." And you know what? There's no telling how this world might have changed if my mother, with her tremendous savvy and Mediterranean bravado, had let her hair down and had gone for the gold.

I learned something on a visit to France about living life to the fullest. On any afternoon, you will see women old enough to remember D-day, sitting together in cafes making a limited-budget espresso last an hour, dressed as if they are ready to meet their lovers—earrings, hair coiffed, vintage good suit or blouse and scarf, a little lace, and makeup—ready for life, because it ain't over till it's over. And you'll see their male contemporaries wearing jackets and ascots, walking their little dogs, looking for all the world like they've just taken a break from an interview with *Le Monde*. All of them could look sloppy in a crinkle-nylon warm-up suit and sneakers, rationalizing that it's easier and it makes no difference because they're not young. But they don't, because they take too much pride in their appearance, and they get just as big a thrill out of dressing with taste now as they did fifty years ago. The moral of the story is that life will sparkle if you will let it—if you will remember that *the bubbles aren't all in the champagne.* If we had as good a grip on aging with respect and sparkle as the Europeans do, we wouldn't even have to talk about this. The bottom line is that we're just going to have to develop an attitude, to get what we want out of every last day of our lives—the last decade of which is just as important and comes with as much potential as the first. Potential, you say, in the last decade? Damn right. There's a great line in the film *Moonstruck*. The college professor says the tender, little female students he has a propensity for dating are "as fresh and bright and full of promise as moonlight in a martini." Be that way. Be your own version of it.

Here are some tried and true means to that end, things to do for you:

Protect Yourself. Life is like a flea market—look for the bargains, have a good time, but KEEP YOUR HAND ON YOUR WALLET. Your wallet is your well-being—emotional, physical, and financial. Assume there's no one else to do it but you.

Listen to What People Say. There is a great commercial for Motorola pagers that features historical characters like Julius Caesar ignoring incoming messages—"Caesar—keep your eye on Brutus. I'll explain later."—and it costs them big. You can learn a lot about yourself from other people. Do they confide in you? Do they emulate you? Do they offer suggestions? How dare the arrogant bastards try to improve perfection!

See Beauty Everywhere. Admit it, even a traffic cop's lapels have a certain interesting symmetry as he writes you a hundred dollar ticket for jumping lanes and doing an illegal U-turn. And those reflective aviator sunglasses are like languid pools, aren't they, as the brain behind them estimates how long it'll take you to post bond. You might as well enjoy it. Look around you—the tops of old buildings, the lines in an old face, the curve of the staircase, the curve of the back of his head as he walks away. Oh hell, all you can do is try.

Develop Your Own Style. You have *great style*. You're a classic, a one-of-a-kind! You show your style in your movement and your words. You know very well how body language works— cross your legs and fold your arms, and you're saying you're skeptical, you're protecting yourself, you can get along on your own. Walk like you own the place, and you have everyone's attention. They don't know whether to love you or worry you're about to buy the joint and have them all fired.

And your wardrobe: What do you want your clothes to say about you? Which "you" will you be today? The way you dress, of course, sends the message that registers first. It's more than an expression of your personality and your mood—it's a tool. Have fun, but use it wisely. Do a little experiment: go to the same store or restaurant twice. First, do that backpacker thing. Then a week later, take the Fendi handbag and wear the Chanel suit. You know the rest. What a difference.

Develop an Attitude. Expect to achieve. Expect to be happy, to be taken seriously, and to be appreciated.

Get a Little Household Help. It may be more affordable than you think, and worth skipping a dinner out, here and there. Ask around. See if you can find someone trustworthy and dependable. It will make you feel better to know that you're placing your possessions in the hands of someone who has a track record with people you know. She doesn't have to be there every day. Having her come in even every other week will keep your place looking nicer, and it'll make you feel like a queen. Ironically, it's also more of an incentive for you to pick up after yourself, since you see it looking stellar when the maid is through, and you realize it really is possible.

Behave Yourself. Don't pick fights you can't win, and understand that if you abuse your body, it's going to get you for it.

Exercise. Choose something you love, or several things that appeal to you. This will enhance your chances of keeping it up. Establish a routine. This will improve the odds that you'll get all your exercise in, before life gets in the way. I find that throwing the workout clothes on as I wake up virtually ensures that I'll drag myself into the room down the hall that houses the machines—and the all-important television-set-with-remote-control that has changed American life as we know it. I admit it's a power trip, holding that clicker. When I was married, my husband used to slide through the channels at Mach one speed and say, "Let me know if you see anything you want to watch." How the hell can I let you know? I'm getting whiplash; it's hard to judge a program by a two-word audition. So now, the clicker is in my very own hand, and the biking goes faster.

Eat the Right Foods. Eat according to the research-du-jour, and use your own common sense. My grandfather, Angelo Evangelista, believed—and told the entire family—that red wine every day would cure almost anything. I think it just made you care less if you were a physical wreck, but there's some value to that, too, don't you think?

Go to the Doctor. Get regular checkups, and go when you feel that something isn't right.

Cultivate Interests. Remain interested in life; be searching and alert. You won't have to do much work here. If you are open to life, it will come to you. And when you decide to take life up on its offer, you can cut your own path, and deviate all you want. Sometimes it's okay to follow the crowd as long as you don't care where you wind up. And it's comforting to know it's okay to ask for directions. Ask, ask, ask. The French word for ask is *demande*. Indeed, *demand* more from life, demand to see all of your world. Though you are not obligated to do anything at all, you do have a responsibility to yourself to consider everything.

Smile a Lot. Some people may think you're nuts, but for all they know you're smiling because you're about to give 'em a big ole hug and pull their shorts up around their ears.

Help Somebody. All these wonderful things you are doing for yourself also place you in a better position to do something for someone else. It's very good for the soul. I have found that those opportunities present themselves without your having to seek them out. For reasons too boring to mention, I did not follow my nursing school education with work in that field, nor did I become a lawyer as I always had wanted. A man once sarcastically suggested that the missed legal career was a big mistake, given my love of the language and my propensity for cross-examination; but all I ever wanted from him was an answer, *any* answer, I swear it. In searching for another line of work—or anything at all that would pay the rent—quite by accident I happened into this broadcasting career through small-town radio. And it wasn't long before I discovered that, not only were they paying me for having more fun than humans should be allowed to have, but I was improving other people's lives left and right with my indignant little exposés of unscrupulous business practices.

Over the years, I found myself doing the kind of investigative reporting at local TV stations that gave attorneys the ammunition to finish the job. The stories, the reports, have gelled into a blurry patchwork. The one I remember the most was the grade-school teacher who had been on involuntary, unpaid medical leave for about two years, because she had made enemies in the school administration. There ensued an apparent effort to "gaslight" her—make her think she was nuts. She stupidly put all the looney events into writing. The next thing she knew, she was pegged a psych case. In the ensuing two years, she sold practically every stick of furniture in her house to finance her legal representation and independent psychiatric exams. The school district doctor said she was crazy; her own shrink said all the pegs were in the right holes.

She came to me with stacks of documents, and it was intriguing, if not daunting. Naturally, nobody who knew anything about this wanted to go on camera with it, if he valued his career. Finally, one did—then another—then her students' very supportive parents, and finally all the pieces fit. We aired the story in a series and she was able to win her case in federal court, with back pay, and more. What an exhilarating feeling for both of us, when she walked into the television station, her head held high and a new light in her eyes, carrying a beautiful yellow mum plant as a gift for me, in appreciation of my efforts. She was the one who had suffered so, and the victory really was hers, for enduring and never losing her faith. If life had not taken all those little twists and turns, and a few jerky realignments, she and I never would have met. We both would have lost something. And I might never have learned personally how fulfilling and rewarding journalism really can be.

Of course, there are simpler ways to effect positive changes in other people's lives. You could take one hour a week to do audio recordings for the blind. Or spend an hour at an old folks home, just talking and laughing. There isn't very much of that there. And it would be good for you, too, on days when you're feeling all done in. Have a look at somebody even older and more tired. It's like peeking through the window of a Jenny Craig diet center on the day before your period—all of a sudden you feel positively svelte. There's always somebody fatter, or thinner, than you.

Love animals? Volunteer at the shelter. Or assist in helping battered women begin a new life. Too close for comfort? Then spend an hour coercing department-store cosmetics counter managers to donate samples to the battered women's shelter. With a cause like that, it's hard for anyone to refuse you. In the summer, go to those big hardware stores and get them to donate floor fans for old people who don't have air-conditioning. My friend, Valerie, does *all* the above and she holds down a job—or perhaps it's the other way around. She's amazing. You don't have to try to keep up with her; just remember that every tiny thing you do will make a big difference for someone.

Monitor Yourself. This means your head, and your heart, and your body. So how are you, today? Are you feeling well? If not, consider doing what the well-known endocrinologist, lecturer, and author Deepak Chopra suggests, as he espouses the Indian healing and health art of Ayurveda: Close your eyes and ask your "self" what's wrong. Perhaps you need more sleep, or something you just ate brought you down. If you do not feel that your body is functioning as it should, address it now. Don't let things build up—they may not go away, and the only person who can identify that uneasy feeling, and ultimately take care of you, is you. You can go through a whole day feeling vaguely off-balance without picking up on it. It just comes over you and ruins what you're doing, making everything not quite right. I have found the cause often is something completely unrelated to the task at hand, and simply identifying it can make all the difference in the world.

To do this, you must be willing to open yourself to the answer, perhaps admitting you feel threatened by something, or are worried about something work-related that's months off. Or it could be the man in your life. Maybe you feel you're not equal to some task—you feel inadequate, or unattractive, or deficient in some other way. There may not be anything you can do about any of it at present, but just identifying it helps you to understand what's going on in your head. And you realize it isn't really that Jethro wants to go to another barn dance Saturday. It's that you're delivering a presentation on downsizing at work next week and it's been rattling around in the back of your mind since you said you'd do it three days ago. That fear is becoming progressively more petulant, messing up rational thought, causing you to alienate everybody you know and even a few innocent bystanders, prompting your staff to refer to meetings with you as "drive-by shootings."

But, if you get used to this monitoring, you'll be able to identify uneasiness as soon as it occurs; you will save yourself, and everybody else, a lot of misery. Then, you can go about trying to fix it, to put your mind more at ease. Sometimes writing these things on a secret little piece of paper makes them appear more manageable, since you can see them in front of you. I've been doing that since the fifth grade, when I locked myself in the bathroom and scribbled it all on notebook paper, then tore it into tiny pieces and buried it at sea.

Take the Time to Nurture Yourself. Take such good care of yourself that it's almost against the law. Whatever you can afford. If you can't hire someone to do it, then do it at home. Facials. Pedicures. Keep that hair touched up, even if you have to do it yourself. It's cheaper that way. Sitting in your own living room with a glass of wine, listening to CDs while the color develops beats driving fifteen miles in the rain to have someone named Cherie spend ten minutes dropping Milano Blonde on your roots and charging you the price of a dinner at the Ritz. There's nothing superficial about this. You're a happier person for it, better able to help other people, and you're certainly more pleasing to the eye. Go for facials, or do them yourself. The face that greets the world should have the best skin possible. Present yourself with your eyes wide open, with an expression of interest. Fake it if you have to, it'll get to be a habit. The rule is: nurture yourself. Feel special, and do *not* feel guilty about these time-outs.

Meditate. Do it for twenty minutes at least once a day. It's a mind vacation without leaving home. It allows you to open the door on all those troublesome thoughts that are kicking around in there, preventing you from concentrating on the task at hand—or just preventing you from really enjoying yourself. The thoughts flow out, sometimes so quickly you want to grab a pencil and make notes about things you couldn't remember before, but that would disturb the flow, so you let it go. Many of these thoughts are the culprits that would have kept you awake when you were trying to sleep, too, so there is a double psychological benefit to meditation. For more on the proven health benefits of transcendental meditation, the book *The Relaxation Response* by H. Benson, M.D., is a good resource. Just thinking about meditation, I suddenly am aware of something I'd vowed to put out of my mind: there's a whole pound of dipping chocolate stashed behind the celery in the fridge. It's hard as a rock because it's so cold, but I know where the hammer and chisel are.

People-Watch. It's wonderful fun! We humans are an odd sort: mostly hairless creatures who cover own bodies in the oddest ways, holding it all together with buttons and zippers, posturing and posing and pretending, strutting and pairing off, sulking and breaking up, acting behind the wheel in ways we're too gutless to act face-to-face, asserting and retreating, showing our teeth in a smile while our eyes reveal what we're really thinking. Where does our sense of humor come from? And why is it that when we find something amusing we laugh instead of, say, scratch our butts? Next time you look at a group of businesspeople in their suits, maybe at the airport, imagine how funny it would be if one of them told a joke and the others, quite expressionless, reached around and furiously scratched their rumps . . . or each other's. Now *that's* entertainment, and it's free.

The Last Straw

Defining moments in our lives can surface at any time, and we can discover a lot about ourselves by observing the ways in which we react to other people. The situations in which we find ourselves can be real learning experiences. It's so important to understand that just because something doesn't work out the way we hoped it would, it does not spell failure on anyone's part. Some things are not meant to last forever. Some events are once in a lifetime, and that's their charm. Some relationships have a shelf life and are not intended to go on and on, and the damage comes in trying to force it. Women agree that they have a greater tendency than men to get sentimental and "stay too long at the fair," giving the benefit of the doubt to people who don't deserve it and to situations that don't warrant it, creating an environment so stressful that some days it's hard to function at all. We all hope we will come to recognize the signs in our own lives that are the tip-off that things are about to go 'round the bend, in time for us to do something about it.

To that end, it can be enormously helpful to plan to take an hour or two to sit down and make a list of the things that you've found difficult to handle over a period of time, and then try to pinpoint the event or the issue that was, for you, the straw that broke the camel's back. Take a pen and paper and look for that camel. Beginning may be a little difficult, but once you start rolling, the thoughts won't stop. You'll probably be pleased to discover you possess a far greater tolerance for adverse circumstances than you realize. You also may notice that there are certain things that are guaranteed to send you right over the edge. Knowing this, you can better control situations as they arise by controlling your own behavior. You still will be free to feel what you feel, and think what you think, but you'll be voluntarily channeling your energy into behavior that will do you the most good. If you won't go this far to work in your own interest, then who will?

Choose a situation, at work or at home, something really irritating. It may be easiest to pick a person with whom you had a long-term relationship that ended in the sort of explosion that set a new record on the Richter scale—something that came to a permanent, irreversible end. As you progress, you also will discover that you can pick up interesting things about yourself from the ways you handle less-disturbing situations. I realize this when I think back on a day at the ice rink, when I experienced that little wave of energy that shoots through you when you suddenly make up your mind. When I took up skating not long ago, I bought figure skates—beautiful, feminine white ones with fluffy, pink terry-cloth blade covers. Every time I picked them up it felt like Christmas morning, and every time I tied the laces together and slung them over my shoulder for the walk into the rink, dressed for winter even though it was July, I could believe I was in a Hans Christian Andersen story. This exciting, new experience was especially important to me because when my family lived in the German Alps when I was a kid, I wanted very much to skate. So my mother hired an instructor, and that man absolutely made me crazy because he would not let go of my hand, ever. I wanted to see what I could do all by myself. I didn't mind falling—it wasn't humiliating to me, and it wasn't a failure, it all was part of the fun—I just wanted to *try*. But he was exasperated that I always struggled to break loose. So after two agonizing lessons, he and Mother agreed that my skating days were over. And they stayed over until I awakened one bright day decades later and decided that I was going to do it anyway. So I walked into a rink and rented skates, and a positively giddy feeling came over me as I slipped and slid from one end of the ice to the other, at liberty to fall and get wet and get cold and maybe even break something. At least it would have happened during a rare, adult sensation of exhilarating freedom!

Gradually, I began to see that the toe picks of the figure skates were getting in the way as I tried to raise a little hell on the ice, attempting hockey stops and other decidedly ungraceful movements that must be the product of seeing the classic hockey film *Slapshot* too many times. The damn toe pick was sticking out in front, as it's supposed to for figure skaters who know what to do with it as they jump and spin and land, but as I lifted my foot it invariably got caught on the ice, sending me ass over tea kettle onto a surface as hard as concrete. This gave me new respect for a water product that heretofore I'd come to think of only in terms of cooling martini glasses and chilling champagne. Also, as I looked around at the other skaters, it seemed to me that the ones who were getting the biggest kick out of what they were doing were the ones in the hockey skates, with shorter, thinner, rocker-style blades designed for greater maneuverability. But I fought off the urge to do something about it, believing I had made a commitment that I had to stick to, whether it suited me or not, and that anything else would be giving up or giving in. Then my "defining moment" arrived. I was practicing the hockey stop—that showy, sideways skid that sprays ice into the air in a most impressive way and makes a really neat *schwooshing* sound—when a very helpful and kind woman who was excellent on the figure skates glided over to tell me that "we always learn the t-stop first." Right then, at that exact instant, I knew I wanted hockey skates more than anything. No rules, no order of business, no judges, no arabesques, nothing but fun, fun, fun, the kind of fun a kid has when the water freezes over on the pond. That very afternoon I got a pair of used hockey skates and nothing has been the same since. Now I skate in full gear and practice hockey a couple of times a week with other women who love to play. If it hadn't been for that last straw, who knows how much longer it would have taken? I am thinking that this particular straw indicates to me that no matter how much effort I put into doing what I think I ought to do, I can't change who I am and I can't deny those measures of independence and freedom that are basic to being me. Does any of that work for you?

Another of my last straws may help to get you going on your list. It arrived the day I came to terms with the fact that my

sweet little German shepherd, Romy, was well past her pup-
pyhood but never would grow past the urge to reduce anything
that would fit in her mouth to rubble, regardless of how many
new-and-improved, ASPCA-sanctioned, veterinary-approved
and kennel-tested chew toys I provided for her. She had de-
stroyed lots of things that meant something, and she just
seemed to have a gift for going for the ones that cost the most:
purses, shoes, clothing, designer sunglasses—everything man-
gled beyond recognition. What's this? I can't identify it. Did
it used to be—oh my God, it's the green shade from the little
brass lamp in the den. Doesn't it hurt to chew on glass? Then
she went really too far. She went to work on the bookcase that
contained my CDs and records, and gnawed her way alpha-
betically through my favorites. It was hard to catch her doing
this, because it wasn't on a regular basis. I began to keep a
diary of her deeds and moods and any events at all that might
help me find the key to the puzzle: full moon (Charles Azna-
vour's Greatest Hits and Bryan Adams); low barometer and
rain (the Beachboys); switched dog food brands (*Cabaret*); the
cat got in the house (the Eagles); Congress couldn't agree on
a budget (Etta James's "Love's Been Rough on Me" and Van
Morrison). There was no pattern and time was running out.
I didn't think I could bear it by the time she got to the Right-
eous Brothers, and I used to sit on the Headline News set at
work and ponder during sports whether she might be dozing
in a corner of the house (camera zoom to her innocent, soft,
fuzzy closed eyes, which fly open Cujo-like) and suddenly
jump up with a craving for vinyl and plastic that would not
be denied.

One night I came home from work to find she had whipped through the Ns, and had gone all the way to the Ss on a canine search-and-destroy mission unheard of in peacetime. Finally she had gone too far: She had demolished my husband's prized, rare, bootleg recording of Frank Sinatra's Birthday Party Roast—the most famous celebrities and cronies from every corner of show business, the real pros, complimenting but, more often, mercilessly humiliating Ole Blue Eyes in the grandest, bawdiest tradition of the roast. And that was it. Romy's moment of truth, and mine. She immediately relocated to a farm with a loving family who would allow her to run and chew till their cows came home; and from this particular last straw, I learned I am a very understanding camel with a pretty strong back, but that a sense of history—and let's face it, dollar value—do carry enough weight in my life to make things happen.

I asked a couple of friends to share their defining moments. One woman lived with a man for a number of years, and thought it would last forever. It did begin in the nicest way, with mutual respect and promises to take good care of themselves in the years ahead, not to try to change the other person, and as much as possible to stay like the person each of them fell in love with. This would allow, of course, for the sort of growth they both hoped would occur emotionally, intellectually, and in their careers. Through the years there were ups and downs. I don't know why he found it hard to live with her, but I do know the things he did that she says kept her constantly into the margaritas—things that were "challenging" but not enough, by themselves, to cause a breakup. After ten years about the only activity they shared was running; and one day he simply stopped, about a block from their apartment, announcing he would do nothing more to maintain good physical conditioning; he'd just had enough. This was his prerogative, but it was a shock to her since she had gone in just the opposite direction and spent hours a week working out. He took to sitting in front of the television for hours and hours, with the remote control that she so grew to detest. One Saturday she stuffed it in her purse before she went shopping, knowing it'd drive him to distraction when he couldn't find it. When she came home, he had taken the couch apart and was racing to get to RadioShack before it closed.

Seeing that they had better begin doing something, *anything* together because they were becoming total strangers, she decided to join him in front of the TV set. When she did, hoping they could find common ground in some sixty-minute special, she couldn't stand it. He never watched anything for long, and if she wanted to watch, he simply got up and left. It all seemed pretty hopeless and the future looked depressingly bleak, but still she stayed.

You know what finally did it? She was lying in bed one night and heard herself telling him again to get up and brush his teeth before he went to sleep. She realized she was married to Beaver Cleaver, a full-grown nine-year-old, and there was just something about that particular thing that was the absolute last straw.

Another friend found her defining moment in bed in a different sort of way. She had been dating a man for about a month and things were moving right along without many of those natural stumbling blocks two people encounter spending so much time together in close quarters. and she felt that they shared something quite special. So after much deliberation, she decided to take their intimacy to a new level—and do him a *really* big favor. She engaged in that sex act that has come to be known, far and wide, as the Lewinsky (no, not the cigar, the other). She thought this would really ring his chimes and she wanted him to see it as a loving gesture, her way of showing him she cared completely. Afterward, much to her surprise, things did not go as she planned. He did not murmur sweet, appreciative nothings in her ear. He sat up brightly and smiled, said something that sounded like "thanks," gave her a quick little peck on the lips, pulled up the covers, turned away from her, and went to sleep. At this point she knew that she was looking at more than fresh material for a letter to *Cosmopolitan.* She didn't stay long enough to think it through—that came later—but she didn't need to get hit upside the head with a 2 × 4 to see that the two of them were a world-class mismatch, and that such a condition is permanent. Feeling wounded and rejected, she got up, got dressed, walked out, and never went back.

You're going to love this one. A beautiful young woman I know was carrying around 250 pounds of weight. She was a size twenty-four. She'd been heavy all her life, and hated it. She tried every diet in the world, and always gained back all the weight she had lost, and then some. She was miserable and completely out of control, because she was addicted to eating. In her words, she was existing without living. Then, something happened. Her immediate family—her father, mother, and two brothers—all were diagnosed with diabetes within a period of twelve months, with weight considered a major contributing factor. And that was her wake-up call. She underwent a surgical procedure known as a gastric bypass—she had her stomach stapled—and in five months lost 130 pounds and now wears a size 5/6. She's healthy and happy and feels like she has been reborn.

Some last straws are found on an automobile ride. It happened that way to a friend at work, who is a tremendous animal-rights advocate. She volunteers at an animal shelter, and she and I have spent much time over the years discussing everything from vegetarianism to boycotting companies that perform experiments on animals. She had just bought a new car, and she and her boyfriend went for a ride. He was driving. A squirrel ran out in front of the car, and he did not attempt to swerve to miss it, or even hesitate to run over it. When that squirrel died, she decided it was bad karma for the car, but worse karma for him. The relationship was over, on the spot.

Her friendship with her best girlfriend met a similar fate when, after sharing all the things close friends share—confidences, talks about life, family, and love—she found out quite by accident that this woman had been sleeping with her ex-boyfriend for over a year and never said a word about it.

Yet another last straw: a sixteen-year-old was dating a married man who was twenty-eight. He told her that he was staying with his wife only for the sake of their daughter, that he and his wife never slept together (well they slept, but they never had sex). And, of course, his wife didn't understand him. My young friend told all this to the mother of another friend, who replied predictably, "That's the same crap men have been telling women for years. They always say that when they're cheating on their wives." And the affair was over, because this particular sixteen-year-old actually listened to what someone told her, and she realized it was absolutely true.

So you can see that from tooth brushing to squirrels to Lewinskys to sixteen-year-old kids dating twenty-eight-year-olds, we all draw the line in different places. Looking at our own history shows us the things that matter the most to us; and if we can take this information to heart, it can set us free to pursue the things and the people that can make our lives more fulfilling and happy, and save us a lot of trouble.

Conway Twitty and Other Regrets

What do you wish you'd done that you didn't do? What did you almost do, almost say, almost have to tuck away and remember?

It seems that of all the things we regret, we feel the worst about the things that didn't take place. If we actually do something and it doesn't work out, at least we can look back and say that hindsight is twenty-twenty and perhaps it should have happened differently, but at least we tried. That's the basis for some of the most enchanting operas, the most haunting poems, the most meaningful plays. It's human nature, it's us.

What did you lie awake and fret over when you were in grade school, besides dropping your books or forgetting to do your homework or losing your gloves or farting in class? Think back. I distinctly remember an event that took place at the end of the fourth grade that so captured my attention and drove me to distraction that I tossed and turned in my sleep for weeks; I remember it to this day with the clarity I usually reserve for Neiman-Marcus "Last Call" sale dates. The last few days of school in Albuquerque, New Mexico, the air was hot and still and filled with the promise of running through sprinklers in the summer, and lying on cool lawns idly obstructing the march of ants with blades of grass, and gulping my mother's Kool-Aid from frosty, gem-colored aluminum tumblers cradled in little hands with short nails carefully painted Babydoll Pink or Azalea Orange. During recess, my girlfriends and I would sit in the shade of the doorway to the school, playing jacks on the concrete. Now as any girl knows, the rubber balls that come with jacks sets are a joke. The serious player will settle for nothing less than the best—the Cadillac of balls—the golf ball. It bounces the highest, and the crisp crack that sounds at each bounce is exhilarating, making your ears perk up like a dog who has heard a shot in the distance. You hear that ball hitting the pavement on an afternoon in May, and you know that the game is on, that the championship contest of the afternoon—perhaps of all time—is issuing you a challenge, calling your name, awaiting an answer.

I had one of those golf balls, and it was a prize. Daddy didn't golf, so I acquired it by trading three extraordinary marbles— an enormous cat's eye with dark amber swirls, and two steelies that must have been dropped by a UFO, because they were weighted in a way that suggested mysterious origins. I never could leave them lying around because the boys tried to steal them. Unfortunately, I left the ball lying around and it fell into someone else's hands three days before school was out. I was devastated. We were living on a shoestring and I didn't even consider mentioning it to my parents. After all, there were ballet and piano lessons, and how much could I ask for?

As you remember, on the last day of school the teacher always tried to clear out the lost-and-found box. Items that were unclaimed went to anybody who wanted them, and this year they were a jumble of weathered lovelies: a beaded moccasin, a red glove, a navy cardigan sweater with holes at the elbows, a pale pink chiffon scarf, a plaid shirt (someone went home without his shirt?), a bracelet of pastel beads, *a golf ball.* Surely someone would come forward for it. But what if no one did? What if she didn't find out until the last minute that her beloved plaything was languishing in the bottom of the box, waiting to be lovingly rescued and taken home? How embarrassing it would be to advance to the teacher's desk to retrieve it, only to be confronted by the rightful owner. The humiliation would live forever.

So I watched as the box was emptied and the teacher at last placed the golf ball on the chalk tray of the blackboard. It sat there all afternoon. I couldn't take my eyes off of it. I memorized every hollow and the way the name stretched across it in red, commanding my attention, taunting me with its availability, demanding to be desired. By the time the bell rang I *knew* that ball, and I knew that it was meant for me. But I said nothing, because it wasn't mine. As I walked home for the last time that school year, I pondered the question of ownership. Wasn't it mine? No one had claimed it, which meant it belonged to no one. And no one else wanted it, or someone would have said something. I considered going back for it, but that would make me late getting home and that was never appreciated. Mother had my travel time calculated doorstep-to-doorstep, and I deviated from that at my own peril. So I spent the first afternoon of that summer lost in thought about that ball. Under other circumstances I would have been lying on the ground in my secret place in the backyard looking at the clouds and happily planning the weekend trip to the neighborhood swimming pool; I could do nothing but poke at the dry, New Mexico dirt with a stick and anguish over the image of the near-perfect white sphere perched on the shelf in the deserted classroom.

By the time I went to bed, I was a poster child for distraction and indecision. By dawn's early light, I had made up my mind to go back and retrieve the ball if it was still there. Mother would've killed me if she'd known that I was venturing back to a deserted school without telling anyone, and it did cross my mind that it wasn't the smartest thing I'd ever done. When I got there the front doors were unlocked and as I ran down the hall not a soul was around. My heart was pounding as I threw open the classroom door and saw that . . . it was gone. It was meant for me, and now it was gone. Someone else had it, someone who surely could not appreciate it as I could, who would not prize it as I would. It was gone, and all because I had not been able to bring myself to say at the end of class, "If no one else wants this, I'll take it."

I remember that incident as a monument to my shyness and lack of confidence. Over the years the experience has prompted me to reconsider some things I was tempted to leave undone, to ask myself exactly why I was making the decision not to pursue them. Because if I was doing it just because of shyness, it was not a good enough reason. We all hope we learn from the past, and often we do; but there is another blunder that stays in my mind and is a constant reminder to me that you're never too old to act like a fourth-grader.

I like all kinds of music and am as familiar with the libretto to *La Boheme* as with all three movements of Beethoven's *Sonata Pathetique* or the lyrics to most any Elvis song or Savage Garden or Etta James. I also like a little country music now and then, and Conway Twitty has always been the biggest favorite of mine, because I think he really sang for women. He knew what we wanted to hear a man say. I am very fond of the way he growled the words, low and sensuous and aching with a sort of teenage longing. To this day, when I hear him sing "Hello Darlin' " I damn near start bawling and faint dead away. I don't know what it is, it's just always been that way. I've had a crush on him for decades. Well, a few years ago it happened that he was going to be appearing on a Sunday morning at a K-Mart in beautiful downtown Lilburn, Georgia, which was right on my way home from doing the *CNN Week in Review* in Atlanta. All week I thought about stopping by with one of my dog-eared albums of his songs and asking him to sign it. Then I thought how silly I'd look. Then I thought I didn't care how silly I'd look, I really just had to meet him and shake his hand and allow myself to be a groupie this one time. (Yeah, like the ones who arrange to accidentally bump into me in one store after another, and reassure me that they're not nuts and they're not dangerous and not possessed by evil spirits and they don't know how the government was able to read their thoughts last night as they sat in the john at home. Christ.) Anyway, I really did want just to tell the man how I loved his music and how it seemed that over the years it reflected the paths of my life. But the week went by and I wasn't really committed, didn't have a plan. Then Sunday came, and on the way back from CNN, I drove by the K-Mart and it was standing room only all the way out into the parking lot, a double queue of women in warm-up suits and the obligatory button earrings and New Balance running shoes and snacks and Thermos bottles, ready for the wait. They were there for the duration. If I had stood in line, by the time I got in, I would have fallen off my cute little high heels and been in such a pissy mood that I'm sure he'd have wished to God I'd just gone home. For the first time in my career, I considered going to the manager of the store, whom I knew, using my "position" to go to the head of the line and spend three minutes with the man I didn't know who had the voice and the feel that for years had lulled me to sleep and soothed my tears after a love gone bad. But I couldn't make myself jump the line, and I didn't do it. I'd see him another time.

Conway Twitty died a year later. I never did get to meet him, and the finality of that is something I think of often, when I'm tempted not to call a friend or write a letter or go out of my way to thank someone for an act of kindness, or when I am about to end a telephone conversation in anger. It just isn't worth it. It also comes to mind when an opportunity presents itself and it's something I'm frankly just too lazy to handle. I don't always take advantage of the opportunity, but I certainly know what the risks are if I pass it up. This is not a bad thing. We ought to be equipped with all the information we need when we make a decision, and the consequences of not taking action are something we need to factor in.

Unfortunately, the only way we are able to see the importance of this is to go through the loss of an experience that really means something to us.

One of the regrets that stings the most is missing out on a love affair because you simply shied away. You were scared that you wouldn't be able to do it right, or that you couldn't give enough.

When I was twenty-one and working six days a week at my first radio station job in Colorado, hundreds of miles from my parents in New Mexico, my mother wrote me a letter chastising me for not being the sort of daughter she thought I should be. She was irritated that I did not visit or call as often as she would have liked. I actually thought I was doing a pretty good job of staying in touch, and remembering special occasions with little gifts and cards.

This was not the first time she had threatened to disown me for some perceived injustice; so I sat down and wrote her a very short letter detailing my simple philosophy about love: *If we want to be loved, then we must be prepared to accept this love in the manner in which it is offered or we can reject it—that's our choice. But we can't change the nature of it, or the way in which it manifests itself.* For instance, if I were inclined to express my daughterly affection only by wearing a lobster on my head once a year on her birthday, Mom should be grateful for it and think of something nice to say. She thought I was being smart with her, and to this day the subject is alive and well. It has gone from being a source of irritation, to providing hours of entertainment and spirited discussion, to what it is now a moot point, since she's figured out I'd never put a lobster through that.

But years later, the words I wrote to my mother returned to teach me my own lesson. I was in love with a man I was convinced was "the right one." There was total acceptance between us and a very deep bond. But it was not possible for us to be together as we wanted to be. After a time, the necessary physical distance between us, and the long hours and nights without him, became too much. I tried many times to sever our ties, but he wouldn't let me forget. I took long drives, even fled to Europe. Nothing worked. His devotion and kindness always brought me back. Finally I decided to make the big break. It nearly killed both of us. I had no desire for food (me, the chocolate queen!). After five days I'd lost four pounds from not eating, I hadn't slept a second, and had developed an ulcer. Every day he saw that roses were left on my doorstep, and he sent little gifts of the heart, things that were special to him, the offerings of a little boy searching his room for treasures to give the girl he loves. Still, I would not allow even communication between us.

I remember thinking one night as I walked to my car after work, "So this is what it feels like to die—to die from the inside out." Through a lifetime of the ups and downs we all experience, I never had felt so depleted, so empty, so lost, so alone. All the tough-girl things I had done meant nothing now; they couldn't help me. I couldn't even meditate. I could only pray for some sort of sign.

Suddenly a serious family crisis emerged—my family—and

quite by accident (or was it?) he called me five minutes after I learned the bad news, and I automatically picked up the phone. He was calling to leave me a message: I should expect to find a magnificent bottle of champagne on my doorstep, and I should retrieve it before someone else did. The sound of his voice on the other end of the line was the music of angels. The relief that swept through me was overwhelming, like being immersed in warm water. He was so concerned about me, about my family's difficulties. He offered his characteristic, sincere assistance. He was, as always, generous with his love and protective devotion to me. He told me what he had told me so many times: that I was not, would never be, without him. He always would be there, always taking care of me, always loving, always ready to help.

Suddenly the words I had written to my mother decades earlier came to me in a flash of insight: if we want to be loved, then we must be prepared to accept this love in the manner in which it is offered.

I acknowledged that I felt that I could not be happy (or healthy) without him, and that the situation could change anyway, making me feel ridiculous that I'd worried in advance over nothing. So I prepared myself to accept his devotion, accept this gift of love, realizing that it was better to be with him than without him.

I knew already it wouldn't be easy, loving at a distance, but this was the direction in which life was taking me. It became so clear that when we resolve not to lose control of our destiny, part of being successful and happy is understanding that there is such a thing as rolling with the punches and making the most of a situation, even when it involves affairs of the heart. When the universe *forces* you to accept something that feels that right to you, you're stupid if you don't *listen to the message.*

There is another lesson that comes out of this. The legendary blues singer Etta James expresses it so well, as she anguishes over the way she feels. Yes, it's a man again that's causing her head to swim and her life to spin out of orbit:

I can't help the way I feel . . . I didn't make myself.

Say this to yourself out loud right now: I can't help the way I feel . . . I didn't make myself. Don't you feel better already? What a load off your shoulders, when you finally allow yourself to admit that you simply cannot help what you are feeling.

A Trip to Your Romantic Side

We're going to take a little trip to the perfect spot for you to begin to explore what's inside you: the lighter side.

An important component of a full life is allowing yourself the giddy, childlike pleasure of planning real adventures—lots of them. Camping and communing with nature are fine and good for the soul. I've always enjoyed seeing relatives, though with the inevitable trauma associated with allowing that many representatives of the gene pool within arm's reach of each other, I don't classify it as a vacation. And there's something to be said for lazing on the beach of an island sipping a Mai Tai. But let's go for something a little more interesting and a little less predictable.

Before the Berlin Wall came down, I used to love to go to Berlin and get a Cinderella pass (a visa that expired at midnight) into Communist East Berlin, crossing over at Checkpoint Charlie. With what they put you through just crossing the border, the adventure began immediately. One day, being an American not used to tolerating the sort of bureaucratic games that were a part of Communist daily life, I decided to end the lengthy waiting at the border after the pre-visa interrogation by *letting myself into the Eastern sector.* I jumped over the waist-high iron gate—right into the arms of two large border guards. This wasn't all that bad, but the Kalashnikov machine guns were a little scary. Thank God they didn't want to do the paperwork associated with shooting up a visiting American and shipping her back in a box; they let me go. That particular visit ended with a Red Army commander escorting me back to the border (voluntarily—he just wanted to show off his English, which really was quite impressive).

You don't have to nearly trigger an international incident to have an adventure. You can, of course, do something even more dangerous—like my wacky friend with a propensity for going into the South American jungle to bring out gemstones. Personally, I prefer healthy-looking border guards and Kalashnikovs to anacondas and native guides with shaky references.

But we must agree that for it to be an adventure, your endeavor must interest you, show you something new, incorporate the element of chance, enhance your self-esteem, and stimulate you in a most pleasurable way. We know already that as a reader of this book you are a fan of the fun side of life, you are interested in people, and there is something deep inside you that really can turn you on, if you'll let it. May I suggest that your adventure be the sort of trip you don't read about in travel books? The sort of experience that says, "I'm here, where I've always wanted to be, to leave everything about the past behind and stay till I run out of champagne/beer/Maalox/money. And I'm going to do this in a way that nourishes my soul and changes the way I'll see life when I go back home." The kind of trip that will light up your life will be carried out with a joie de vivre that is exclusive to the French. I urge you to make up your mind to indulge in . . .

Romantic Travel the French Way or, Let's Get the Hell Out of Here!

Your own personal romance can be anything you choose. There are many kinds. You can have a love affair with a city, a painting, a feeling, a way of life, or a person. You're going to get more out of this trip than twelve rolls of undeveloped film and an American Express bill so big you can hear it coming down the street.

It's not about money, it's about attitude. It begins with a frame of mind that is uniquely French. It invites adventure, and an attitude that appreciates the romance, the humor, the possibilities in just about everything. It's "La Vie en Rose"— life through rose-colored glasses.

When you're preparing for your journey, toss practicality right out the window. Figure out the new subway passes later. When I'm packing, I make it an event! I stand across the room and with reckless abandon, throw into the suitcase only the things I love, things that make me feel *fabulous* when I'm wearing them including, of course, impractical little lacy numbers.

A few weeks in advance, hang out at the Alliance Française in your city and learn the French phrases you need to make life interesting. Alliance Française is a nonprofit school with branches all over the world. I've been studying there as time permits for years, hoping one day on a visit to France to be mistaken for a local, or at least for a European with a bad accent. I have learned to fake the Gallic version of subjunctive and indicative, which is quite an achievement considering I don't even know what the hell they are in English.

Ask visiting or resident French men and women what the locals do to have fun. They may suggest you watch the sun come up from a private vantage point high above Paris, spend a lazy afternoon at a cafe where meeting members of the opposite sex is guaranteed, or catch that magic, late-summer moment when the sun sits on the Arc de Triomphe just before it dips into the night. And ah, the night! The world is glittering at your fingertips.

I have a Parisian friend who bribed the lady at Notre Dame to let him take a date up there where the gargoyles dwell, after dark, for a romantic interlude overlooking the City of Light. The French pride themselves on their creativity, and issuing them a challenge can be very interesting.

Then there is the American woman who, in one week, learned a lesson that changed her life. It came in two parts, which she says I can share with you: 1. *You don't have to be beautiful or handsome to be admired.* Exude style of your very own—no one can duplicate it—and an unabashed interest in life and other people. 2. *Flirting is free, and it's okay.* What a great confidence boost, whether it's in France or in the States. Sure, you'll shock some guys when you do it back home, but maybe they need shocking, and anyway, what's the worst that can happen? You stumble upon a man who turns out to be married, and his wife shows up at lunch in an expensive restaurant, and *mon dieu*! She causes a scene, dumps hot coq au vin in his lap, and he flees. In which case, you are left with a superb bottle of Brouilly, which now you have all to yourself—unless, of course, that gentleman over there . . .

What is it about American women that makes us so ambivalent about even casual contact with the opposite sex? We certainly invite it—doing our hair and makeup in the most attractive ways our time and money will allow; yet, when a man pauses to take it all in and cast us an appreciative glance, we get all pissed off.

In France, "appreciation" is the key word—appreciation of members of the other gender, regardless of social status, economic status, or age—along with the general feeling that we all had better enjoy today, because tomorrow isn't even a promise. Example: On a recent visit to Paris, on a windy, drizzly January afternoon in a lovely cafe just outside the Palais Royale, I left the table to seek the toilette, and found it in a little room downstairs, where many of them are in restaurants. In that room were two cubicles with solid doors, one for men and one for women. Everyone shared a small sink and mirror. I was touching up my makeup when a very good-looking man emerged from behind a door and began to wash his hands. As I looked down, I could feel him watching me in the mirror. So I decided to have a little fun. As I applied my lipstick very slowly, I raised my eyes even more slowly until they met his . . . and he didn't even blink. His beautiful, brown eyes looked deep into mine as he held my gaze, and we shared a delightful, intimate moment that seemed to last half an hour but couldn't have been more than fifteen seconds. I put away my lipstick, he smiled, and I smiled. I left and never saw him again. It was a lift you can't buy on a rainy day.

Maybe it's the rain that brings out the Romper Room in the French male. On another trip, by the time I'd been in Paris exactly one hour and a half, I had been accompanied off the RER train line that links Charles de Gaulle Airport with *centreville*, the center of town, by a very nice man who had struck up a conversation by asking to see my Metro (subway) map and then remained interested after the ride; I had been assisted by another gallant man in lugging my suitcases up endless flights of stairs at my Metro stop; this one wanted to get together during my stay. And a waiter at an outdoor cafe at the Tuileries gardens by the Louvre had brought me a dear little first bloom of spring that had fallen from a tree, as my own waiter winked and literally danced a few feet away. I don't know what inspires this kind of lighthearted behavior, and I don't care. Rain? The air? Six weeks without getting laid? I don't know, and it doesn't make any difference. It's the kind of thing you want to seal in a Baggie and take back home, for those numerous slow, boring days when everybody takes everybody else way too seriously.

There are a few things women should know about chance meetings with men in Paris:

1. They will happen whether you want them to happen or not.
2. A woman telegraphs her interest in the opposite sex, whether she's interested in the particular recipient of

these signals or not. It's the body language and the attitude. If you're short on one or the other, nature seems to compensate.

3. Don't be afraid to be friendly in response to courteous overtures. If you smile and say hello, this does not commit you to marriage. Paris is the only city I know in which a woman can have an intimate relationship with a total stranger, without their even touching, while she's waiting for a sandwich. So don't feel terribly threatened by eye contact. It's part of the natural flirtation with life.

4. Don't be afraid to ignore him or even openly get rid of him. It's the chance he takes. Parisian men can make such a game of pursuing you, even when you're clearly not interested, that you may have to take drastic measures to let them know you're not in the mood. One November night I was in a movie theater, prepared to make a bit of work watching a film with Italian dialogue and French subtitles, when an absolutely gorgeous man sat next to me and flashed a knowing smile just as the lights went down. I smiled back out of reflex and already knew his game was on. I wondered what he had read into my smile. Keep in mind, I had been standing outside in the icy wind in a queue with other ticket holders for forty minutes, waiting for a seat for the late show, alone— not keeping warm by smooching as two-thirds of the others had been doing. And I looked like hell and was frozen to the bone. I did not feel attractive at all.

Apparently that is not a prerequisite when it's pushing midnight.

I must be the most naive female on the planet. About half an hour into the movie it felt as if a moth were flapping around my knees. I looked down and saw his hand sort of playing with the seam of his jeans, and his knee was very close to mine. I moved mine away a bit, and pulled my long, leather coat over it. A few minutes later, the coat had slipped off and he was at it again. I moved again, and he pursued. I looked at him—I had to smile, I couldn't help it—and said, "You don't give up, do you," at which he laughed with delight, making eye contact that was impossible to ignore. I pulled up my coat again, and settled in to watch the rest of the movie. Ten minutes before the end, he blatantly put his hand on my knee. At this moment the award-winning film, *Life Is Beautiful*, was dealing with the most frightening aspects of the Holocaust, and I thought that for him to make such a move at that time took gigantic balls. I didn't have access to them, but I did have his hand within easy reach. I placed mine on his, looked up meaningfully into his dancing, horny eyes, delicately wrapped my fingers around his little finger, and slowly pulled it back till I heard it snap in the quiet theater. I thought he took it rather well. He leaned away and sat quietly until the credits rolled, and he wasn't laughing anymore. Then I left before he did. I really hated to have to do that, but a man needs to exercise a little intelligent judgment about playing his game, even in Paris.

Other occasions may require less drastic measures, and words only. "Piss off" might be a little strong at first. You may want to go with "I don't want to talk." You can advance to "My father will have you killed," which works well for women of virtually any age.

5. Evaluate him.

- Wedding band? This may not mean a thing to him one way or the other, but it's a nice bit of information.
- Neatly groomed and well-dressed? So was Ted Bundy, but it's a starting point.
- Money? At least enough to buy you dinner. Food is good.
- Good color in his face? A prison pallor is hard to take when the lights go up.
- Could you fall for him? Careful, honey—you want to *ride* the taxi, not *buy* it.

6. Trust your first impression. The happily ever after in the movie *French Kiss,* between Kevin Kline's sleazy character and Meg Ryan's naive American tourist was a fairy tale. If you get the willies—that brief, unsettling feeling—when your eyes first meet, that's it. Forget everything else about his evaluation. He didn't pass the stress test.

7. Learn the art of walking fast/evading. You may have to shift to overdrive, to get away from some spacey,

wild-eyed character who is pursuing you up and down the aisles of a crowded little grocery store, picking up speed as you take the corners. The two of you are jockeying your little hand-held plastic grocery baskets with the jars of artichoke hearts and caviar rolling around (that's *your* basket—his has the mayonnaise and canned spaghetti). At a time like this, you will find that quick bursts of speed can serve you well and be unnerving to a guy to whom "speed" has an entirely different meaning. And you will learn that the art of hovering comes naturally to a woman with a mission such as yours. You remain motionless, just inside an aisle, as you peruse the offerings across the way. He can't see you, but you know he's there—somewhere—looking for you. And you know with the calm assurance of a warrior, that by the time you're ready to show yourself and leave, either he will have given up or you'll be ready to slap him into next week.

(As I write this by the window in a little cafe on the Champs-Elysées at 10:00 on Friday night, with the activity on the avenue just cranking up, a very good-looking man who appears to be normal is staring intently at me from a table five feet away. If I look up, he'll want to talk and there goes the writing for the night. What should I do?)

That reminds me, if you go out alone in hopes of meeting someone interesting, take paper and a pen. You may need to pretend you have a writing assignment. This also provides a good excuse for not talking if you don't want to. Make copious notes, even if you're only jotting down the Declaration of Independence or what you can remember of the preamble to the Constitution. Otherwise, you'll look like you're there for exactly what you're there for. (*He just ordered a simple cafe sandwich. Somehow that is disappointing, although I knew when I walked in here that it wasn't Regine's. It's rough when they turn out to be human. Still, if you were open to just a fun evening, knowing full well you're going back to the States soon and will be forced to leave Jean-Paul/Luc/ Claude behind, you could have a nice little time—and that, after all, is the whole point,* n'est pas?)

8. Do you smoke? Would you like to? Now, don't get all upset over this. If you're sitting in a cafe anywhere in Europe, you're going to inhale enough second-hand smoke to choke the winner of every Triple Crown from now till it's over. So you might as well consider the fact that there's something inescapably sexy about the way a cigarette languidly burns down and the smoke curls through the air while you have it casually cradled between your fingers as if you couldn't care less. You can do that all day. And a *tiny* drag is not going to turn you into a Gauloise addict, trust me. In college as I studied to be a nurse, I gave up the university smoking habit for good the day I saw a diseased lung in class. So you know I'm not trying to lead you down the garden path. Just keep

the damn thing away from your clothes. The dry cleaning bill will break you.

9. Don't expect the men to be tall. A man's height really isn't an issue, it's just that it was such a surprise. It came to me as I found myself for the first time in the passport check-in line at Charles de Gaulle airport on a Saturday morning. It isn't really a line, it's a sea of humanity, very unhappy humanity who just got off a seven-hour flight from the States and who want nothing more than a hot shower, a couple of hours' sleep and four little words: "Your room is ready." I'm rather tall, 5' 9" and as I waited I noticed that I was eye level with only four or five French men in the crowd. Just remember, it's not what you've got, it's what you do with it. Look at Napoleon. He was so good, they named a pastry after him.

   (*He's writing something on a napkin now, and, seeing that my wine is gone, is trying to summon the waiter. Thing is, he hasn't been very aggressive about it. In fact, he's ordering just another beer for himself.*)

10. The shoes are the dead giveaway. Learn how to peg the wearer as American or European. It's a fun game and a time-saver, if you really want to spend time with a local. Before we go any further: If you feel out of place as you stroll the Champs Elysées in your white K-Swiss tennis shoes, you'll want to stop into a great little shoe store, Andre, and they'll fix you right up with those black shoes with klunky high heels that you see everywhere and somehow grow

attached to. If you watch Europeans' shoes, you can even narrow it down to East or West. The kind that are sort of Oxfords and tie high in the front, like the ones the nuns wore when you were in grade school, definitely are on European feet. And if they have those squishy soles that electrical engineers love, that give you an irresistible urge to stuff leaky ballpoint pens in your fashionable wash-and-wear shirt pocket, the guy probably is from the East. But you could cut him some slack, because he's trying.

And of course in warm weather, sandals make it just too easy. European men will wear socks with sandals, when a guy from Chicago not only wouldn't wear those sandals but would blind anyone who saw him wearing socks with them. (*He just passed the note to me:* "Je ne veux pas vous deranger, mais j'aimerais bien passer ce soir avec vous." *Translation: "I don't want to disturb you but I'd like very much to spend this evening with you."*) This leads us to the final point:

11. It is *your* evening. Be judicious about your decisions, and selective about your company. Sometimes it's enough just to be asked. ("Non. J'ai un headache. *Yes, tomorrow night too.*")

12. If you want to be taken for a resident, walk around with a black leather folder. I don't know why, but Parisians just seem to love these things. God knows what they keep in them. But it's better than carrying a plastic shopping bag, which you ought to hide right

away in that nice black leather satchel that you trucked all the way from Hoboken just for this.

13. Don't even think about actually wearing those fabulous spiky heels you see in the Charles Jourdan window out on the street. You'll be a cripple in an hour. You can slip them on after you reach your destination. Men are used to seeing women in flats.

Speaking of store windows, I still am trying to figure out who is wearing those colorful little nothings that look so appealing on the mannequins on Rue Faubourg-Saint Honore, the very high class, very expensive shopping street near the very high class, very expensive hotels. In this city, black is the word—black and neutrals, year-round.

There is no bad time of year to go to Paris. I spent New Year's '97 there, and the weather that week was nuts. One day it was summer, the next day the rain and the wind blew through, slamming the French windows of the hotel room open so violently in the middle of the night that I vowed to go to church the next day. Yet, all of it was an experience, a passing moment on the Parisian tableau. The chambermaid who mopped up in the morning suggested that the wind, that sudden, frightening tempest, had happened a thousand times before and would happen a thousand times again, and it was nothing to worry about.

When you have spent several days with that casual, pragmatic attitude about things you can't help anyway, you will have learned the important French—European, really—art of taking life a day at a time. Perhaps it is inspired by centuries of incursions, insurrections, monarchies, and liberations. The people are very good at adopting a healthy "wait and see" attitude. This talent will serve you well when you return to the States. By then, you'll have experienced life as it was meant to be lived—easy, nonthreatening, *delightful*—and you will have learned a few things about yourself, and your willingness and ability to let yourself go a bit. As you board the plane with a song in your heart and a stack of credit-card receipts in your wallet, you'll vow to keep that feeling of freedom, that joie de vivre. This plane will carry fellow vacationing Americans, and a few French going to the States on business or vacation or to visit relatives. And you'll probably notice right away that something about this flight is different from the flight into France: There is more English spoken, and the air of anticipation is missing. Don't let it get to you; it's to be expected. Then, about two-thirds of the way through the trip, you'll see something else happening, and this is the sad part: As you sit watching that cute little moving illustration on the wall in front of you, the one that shows your plane approaching the U.S. mainland, you can't help but wonder if maybe it all was just a lovely dream. And you'll swear you can feel the cabin pressure changing as everybody's asses start to get tighter. The worrying sets in again, the seriousness. The scarves that women had knotted about their necks with careless abandon are redone to more exacting specifications or they come off altogether. The laughter isn't lilting anymore, and it's more guarded.

Do not, under any circumstances, feel that you have to fall

into this trap! Don't believe that it ever has to happen to you. *You*, after all, are still back in Paris, because your attitude has been altered, which means your life has changed. It's your choice, and you choose to do it differently now.

No one is suggesting that this is going to be a piece of *gateau* (cake). All around you, friends, relatives, and business associates won't understand the transformation and will try to get you back on the straight and narrow. Consider explaining it to them another time. Right now, it's crucial that you surround yourself with all the wonderful little things you brought back with you—right down to the matchboxes from the hotel, which you place in a bathroom to be used to light candles so that the European atmosphere you so loved will always be with you. Or put the matches on your kitchen or dining room table, for lighting the candle that now always will be glowing during your mealtimes—morning, noon, and night.

Play the music of France. Not the cafe music, but the French rock and Edith Piaf favorites that you bought in the enormous Virgin Records store on the Champs—whatever appeals to *you*. Because it's *your* life. And who knows, you just might expose other people to something that will enrich their lives, as well.

The Virtues of Garter Belts

Assuming you now have returned from your trip to Paris, you undoubtedly have come to understand why you've heard so much about French lingerie, and why American companies try to duplicate it. It's beautiful. You can take the self-transformation you began on your voyage undercover, by jumping into the lingerie game here at home. This is dangerous territory, but you're playing by your own rules so you have the advantage.

Whatever obsession is, I bet love is the same thing. Is it irrational? A powerful attraction that defies logic? Yes, that's it, I recognize it. That's the way I feel about garter belts and stockings. I just love them. I love shopping for them (especially that part) and wearing them under business suits in front of unsuspecting people who think they're looking at a practical, button-down kind of woman. This, of course, automatically eliminates those who know me, and know better. But even those people would be astonished at the number of women who love to walk down the street knowing they've done a little something extra for themselves, something voluntary, a secret female perk that can make PMS and even motherhood a little easier to handle. Show me a day of missed appointments, kids who've lost their shoes, traffic from hell, and a haircut so bad you know your stylist has three 6s on his neck and I'll show you an opportunity to take your existence to a new level, with 20 minutes of trying on lace garter belts in Victoria's Secret.

For so long, we American females have been blissfully ignoring *la belle différence* and its accompanying underpinnings. Our underwear drawers—a mélange of unmatched, grade-school cotton underpants and sensible bras—have become a tiresome salute to androgyny. Well, I'm not saluting anymore, damn it, I want to have some fun. I want to lunch with a friend at a classy little restaurant and, as the waiter pours the merlot, giggle over the enormous sum I just dropped at the lingerie shop on things I can't even throw in the washer, things that go together, fragile little nothings with an indefensibly short shelf life, things my father, who grew up with eight other kids on a farm and always watched a penny, would have said were not sturdy or durable enough (he said that about my swimsuit, in the tenth grade). "Durable" is what linebackers are when they're over thirty-five. I don't want durable. I want sexy! *Sensuous!* I want *"I-want-to-live-till I die" gorgeous* things to wear, and I want them *now!*

Not everyone considers this a sign of a healthy mind. It comes as no surprise that the Internet is adrift in chat groups that explore the perverse joys of Garter Belts and Stockings. And it has been suggested to me that this is proof that GBSs now are only for people who are up to no good. Well hell, Mr.

Bakker, you can make an all-American jar of Mom's Home-style Peanut Butter a sex toy without too much effort, am I right?

I know, you see, why *women* are back to GBSs. It's the Three Ss: secret, special, and sexy. But why do *men* find them absolutely mesmerizing? They cost the tiniest fraction of a set of golf clubs or a motorcycle or twenty shares of IBM. What is it that will propel a man to tell you, in a studied, offhanded way, "Love that outfit you're wearing," when you know there's a lot more going on in his head, because this person, who has seen you in every possible unflattering mode for years, suddenly has the look of a deer caught in the headlights at night. *What is it?*

I went in search of an answer. The men I asked, who are intelligent and good at words when it comes to computers and automobile maintenance, said they didn't know. Liars. A fellow on the Internet suggests that GBSs are, for the male, the perfect combination of gadgetry and sex. If that's true, then I suggest that the only improvement might be to sew a remote control on the garter belt, to make it the ultimate Male Game Station.

Let's return to the other dimension to consider in the wearing of lingerie: the confidence and the fun you gain from wearing something *you know will not be seen.* This is the Thinking Woman's clothing advantage. Many women find they think best when they wear a particular type of outfit or a certain piece of jewelry or when they wear their hair a special way. It's the comfort factor; they are comfortable with themselves and consider themselves in their own element.

How do *you* think best? I have found that I do most bill paying, phone calling, planning, and even writing in my night-gown. Summer or winter, robe or no robe, it doesn't matter. I just feel very comfortable that way. If I were chairman of the board, and in a position to do whatever eccentric thing I pleased, I'd sit at all board meetings in a nightgown with my contact lenses replaced by glasses, and a cup of cappuccino and my favorite pens in front of me. Probably, my hair would be popped into a high ponytail and I wouldn't even be wearing shoes. *Then* I could think. And wouldn't it be wonderful if everybody else at that conference table were doing that pajama party thing. Get rid of those power ties and monogrammed shirts and other status symbols, and get down to business comfortably.

At this point you're expecting me to tell you I wear nighties to work. Well, yes, I do. There are days when I just feel really comfortable in a little short thing that may have been created for the bedroom but can serve an entirely differently purpose, so I just tuck it under my suit jacket and skirt as if it were a slip, and off I go. There is absolutely nothing wrong with this. Who makes up the rules, anyway? They can corral us into wearing tweed on the outside, but they'd better stop there. What we do with the rest of it is our own business.

Obviously, you want to be taken seriously at work, so there are some things you definitely won't wear where they can be seen: like see-through anything, skirts so short they change the weather (unless you bring along the opaque stockings, good shape, and the serious-but-worldly attitude that can make it work), or tops cut so low the men in your office are mentally painting landscapes on your breasts. These things will be self-defeating because they will get you *so much* attention that nobody will hear or care about what you're saying. And you'll piss off every straight woman in the room, at which point you can consider "networking" strictly a broadcasting term.

There are certain concessions we all have to make, whether we're working in an office setting or reading the news on television. You should use your own judgment about what works best. There are little things you can do to change the de rigueur outfit to make it your own. Of course, in the United States we have less latitude than women have in Europe, unless we don't mind spending half the day explaining that *it's okay that you can see lace through the slit in my skirt. It's called "real life," hello.* Personally, I consider it an opportunity to enlighten the more bored/boring sector of the business world. But I get such a kick out of the lady from Des Moines, who quite kindly calls every once in a while to ask that someone in the newsroom drop me a note to tell me that my slip is showing, when she can see a touch of lace under my suit where she might expect to see a high-necked white shirt, like the one worn by Sister Mary Reginald-who-dragged-me-through-sixth-grade, or the sort of open collar number that transforms a news anchor into a Century 21 agent. (That's fine if you happen to be one, but I bet they can't wait till quitting time rolls around.) In a sense, whatever we wear to work is our uniform. Maybe you work out of your home and your uniform is jeans and a sweatshirt. Me, I'm a storyteller filling you in on what's happening in your world. I'm not an intellectual, I just play one on TV. And I dress for it. My uniform, my attire, is "business," the ever-present suit jacket. I wear the suit for everyone else. The lace is for me. It's my own little fashion statement, a trademark. Hardly scandalous. I'm female and I see no point in trying to hide it. I choose to get the most enjoyment out of it.

There are tricks to dressing to be you, while continuing to color between the lines like a good girl. The really uplifting news is that while you're doing this you're probably saving money. The little personal touches you add turn out to be varying combinations of the same elements of your wardrobe. It's very European to resolve never to wear an outfit the same way twice in a row. Before you say that I am not practicing what I preach on the air, let me explain that quite often what works outside the studio is a disaster on camera. Jewelry so shiny under the lights that it could hypnotize everybody in the newsroom into believing that there won't be rumors of another CNN takeover for at least a month, or a blouse that absolutely must be covered with the right jacket because its vertical stripes are so close together the camera makes them dance, prompting everybody from Master Control to your living room to break out the beach music.

Now about those little touches. Here's an easy one: Find a suit jacket, a blazer, that you probably should have had altered through the middle because when you button it, it's so big it makes you look like Mike Ditka. Dig through your jewelry and find a decorative pin, and place it at the center back of the waist. Position it to take up some of the slack, adjusting it till you like the way it looks from the front. And voilà, you have created a one-of-a-kind look. Next week you may decide to belt the jacket or give it to your sister. But today, you're exercising your right to have fun with your wardrobe and do something different in a quiet sort of way.

If you're going out for the evening and are used to wearing slacks, go through your closet and look for a plain dress that could be enhanced with the simple addition of stockings with seams. Or try adding my own favorite wardrobe accessory; a great pearl choker, or one in jet, or goldtone. They can be very flattering. Or be daring at night and wear a lovely blouse with the buttons in the back, fastening only the top one or two. People will stare? Of course they will. Do you want to be noticed or ignored? Do you want to enjoy the freedom of dressing like the individual you are, or stay mired in other people's ideas of what good dressing is? If you want to be ordinary, wear a raincoat and jeans everywhere. If you want to spark a little interest, have a little fun, then do something a little different.

This is easier: Any day of the week, take a fabulous scarf and tie it low on the shoulder strap of your purse. Or braid a couple of scarves and wear them around your wrist. I have a passion for beautiful scarves, yet I refrain from putting the busiest of them near my face. They can compete with a woman's features and confuse the issue. But if you do it right, if you don't rock your universe with a lot of fluff around your neck, and know to wear your scarf gently tucked low like a blouse under your suit jacket, or holding your hair back in a ponytail, I think you can make a statement about your willingness to do things a little differently from everyone else. It shows you're an individual, a woman who is sure of herself and is prepared to take a little wardrobe chance here and there for the sake of experimentation and exploring the possibilities in her world. Not everyone will like what you do, but that's fine because you aren't living for them. On the other hand, if you get to work and absolutely everyone thinks everything about the way you look is perfect, *run*, do not walk, to the nearest bathroom and change something immediately. Button a button or unbutton one. Roll up your sleeves. Take off the cardigan and throw it over your shoulders. Shake your head so that something, for God's sake, is out of place.

The most important thing you can do is try to see every piece of your wardrobe as if you're looking at it for the first time. Try to imagine other ways you can wear what you have, before you go out to buy more.

The next most important thing you can do is wear whatever you've come up with, with the most confidence you can muster. Be genuinely charming and sure of yourself (I promise it will get easier every time), and the people you spend time with will wonder why they never thought to do what you're doing. Even if their critiques clog the office E-mail, they will secretly envy the guts it took you to do it and your determination to be your own person.

How to handle life with dangerous lingerie:

It's important to understand that the lovely little undies we choose are first of all for us. Otherwise, my God, imagine the dollars we'd be spending on the men. Imagine that, when an affair went sour, we'd be tossing out our favorite little slip because it reminded us too much of "him."

Yet, we must be aware that the fate of our favorites sometimes is beyond our control. A friend tells me that her lover once threw out her favorite black lace teddy because his fiancée was on the way to his apartment, and she left it behind in her haste to avoid a confrontation with the bride-to-be, who preferred to go through life in white cotton undies and a training bra. When he saw the teddy, despite his otherwise controlled demeanor and above-average intelligence, he nearly wet his pants like a preschooler when his pager delivered the message that his fiancée was two minutes away. He could think of nothing to do but put the lingerie in the trash. He had hoped my friend would forget, but no woman is going to forget *that*. She asked about it and when he delivered the bad news, he paid. He also paid in dollars.

Also remember that when you make yourself memorable to a man, you place yourself in the same category as his best golf score. He *wants* to take out an ad in the *New York Times*. Men talk, my mother told me, and she was right. In spite of themselves, many men do love to compare notes, once they get past that initial week or so of loyalty to the lady, or when the affair is over, whichever comes first. And certain women live in fear that cute little distinguishing characteristics they have added to their lingerie (and to their bodies) may come up in the course of conversation. Almost like a movie, you imagine your lovers gathered at your graveside, engaged in casual discussion. Each man thought he would be the only one, but so many of them show up for the untimely burial, it turns out they have to take a number. One of them mentions the cute little claret bow on the back of your ivory silk thong teddy. Another, the dainty LIVE FREE OR DIE tattoo you had placed on your frame when you dated a biker, and the one that says DIVERS DO IT DEEPER from your days with the SCUBA instructor. The point is, be careful with the details. They'll get you if you let them.

Some of the most dangerous lingerie you'll ever find is on a street named after a saint. There is an enormous sex shop in Rue St. Catherine in Montreal—the same street where upscale boutiques are situated. No one thinks anything about it. There are lots of sex shops there—and nice cafes and brand-name department stores and girlie joints. In autumn it's not unusual to see teenagers sitting on the sidewalk after school discussing rock music, while across the street somebody named Janette is bumping and grinding her heart out for some book salesman from Chicago who, it will turn out, does not have change for a twenty.

The huge sex shop is called Seduction—and the way it's set up, Sister Mary Euphemia, who ushered me through the ecumenical minefield of Catholic school, could walk in without being shocked out of her shoes. Closest to the door, you find regular lingerie-store-type merchandise and swimsuits. You realize this is not your ordinary ladies' department when, as you venture a few steps further, the swimsuits sprout sequins and the teddies become costumes and it's eight months to Halloween. The interesting thing about this whole setup is that you can feel comfortable going in as a couple or by yourself, regardless of gender, proclivity, or party affiliation.

Next, you find yourself in the ha-ha section, where you see

cutesy little things to take home to everyone on your gift list—at least that's what you tell the helpful people who work there. Everyone is *so* matter-of-fact that if you act the slightest bit embarrassed under their steady gaze, *you're* the one who looks nuts. *They* act like you're buying a new set of tires. I've seen a Seduction employee take a lot of time to explain the pros and cons of those little, rubber bandlike male sexual aids to a customer, all the time pulling and stretching them, damn near using them as slingshots.

So you wander the aisles and become aware that you now have entered The Land of Realistic Penises, which—if you turn right instead of left—will put you right at the leather and latex room. And, oh, you want to see what's in there, since you've already placed your homebody reputation—and maybe a relationship or two—in jeopardy, because God knows which of those English-speaking customers over there knows you from across the border. But you resist the urge to go in because what if there's an alarm on the door?

In the Land of Realistic Penises you come face-to-face with things you never wanted to see: models of every color and size, every shape and texture. Some look positively *bionic* and you start to sweat just because of the proximity. Should a girl from Newark be so near? This area gives way to magazines and blow-up dolls and videotapes.

Mon dieu, the videotapes. There are big signs so you can't get lost: Fetishes, Français, Bisexual, Hetero, et cetera. Now, the trick is not to stray into the wrong section. There are no lines of demarcation, no firm borders. Yet you look up and see that while you were nonchalantly taking in the back of a tape you're holding, you have strayed into dangerous "men with breasts who like to do it to themselves" territory. You hop back two feet like you're doing the Electric Slide, wondering if anyone who happened to see you will appreciate your firm course correction and report same back home in Belleville.

I'd made the commitment to take the entire tour, and had by now removed my sunglasses. I was collecting footage, imagining what the folks in Atlanta would say to gifts titled "Screw You!" "Stockholm Girls," and "Handy Men and Their Tools." I was trying to be inconspicuous in my miniskirt, which now seemed an advertisement, and my Fendi shoulder bag, which suddenly felt like a Well-to-Do-Perverted-American-Woman flag. I had ascended the steps to the upper level of the tape gallery, keeping a wary eye on the big classification signs, reassured that I was concealed by large pillars, but concerned that men directly below me were spending more time looking up my skirt than at the racks. In an effort to move away from them, I backed into a life-size standup of some almost-dressed porn queen and saved her—and me—from diving over the railing by dropping my tapes and grabbing her by the mammaries. *Everyone* looked. I would not have been surprised to hear a loudspeaker announcement for "Cleanup on aisle 5." But the panic passed and when I looked down again everyone had gone back to what they were doing—everyone save a fat little Quebecer who was looking directly at me as he tossed around tapes in a big "sale" bin, muttering that they were low-quality "garbage," as if I had a special insight into such things. After all, I *had* grabbed her *there*.

I made my way cautiously, sideways like a crab, along the

wall, passing titles like *Alone But Not Lonely on the Night Shift*, the plot of which was an obvious waste of time, but I was delighted to see that for once, such an exercise in self-gratification was not at taxpayer expense. A tape jacket caught my eye (no, you have to guess what it was) and it took some effort to pull it off the shelf, sandwiched as it was between other meaningful tales of humanity on the edge. Well, wouldn't you know the whole damn row of tapes came crashing down: Ukrainian liaisons, Asian fantasies, and American big-breasted blonde dream girls, all in an uncoordinated cacophony of arms and elbows and well-explored Grand Tetons and virgin Grand Canyons, all over that nice, neutral Canadian floor. Once again I looked down and everyone looked up. I am not pulling your leg when I tell you that I saw in their eyes a look that screamed, "Better you than me, stupid!" as they headed for the cash register. I was considering pretending someone else had done it, when a Seduction employee brought me a handy plastic basket to make my shopping easier.

When at last I dug into my wallet for the cash—I was *not* going to have a credit-card bill for this come back to haunt me after I got home—I mumbled something about how after a while it all starts to look the same. I'd been there for over an hour—a few more minutes and they'd have asked me to tea. The guy didn't even crack a smile, he was so cool; he also was busy frisking an embarrassed American businessman by the door, someone else who wished to Christ that this afternoon he'd gone to the movies.

———

Interesting, by the way, that we Americans appreciate sex, but we have our priorities and it isn't *the* pastime.

Durex condoms has released the results of a fourteen-country survey on sex and other diversions. Ten thousand people were asked what they'd rather do, given several attractive options. Sex did not come out on top. Close, though. Americans made love an average of 148 times a year in 1997. Only the French did it more, 151 times. Apparently there was no effort to measure the enjoyment: the EQ, or Ecstasy Quotient. I mean, how could you? It's strictly subjective, and anyway someone once pointed out that there is no such thing as a bad orgasm. But then, that would be assuming that all of the above encounters ended in that happy state, and that probably isn't true—at least for a certain gender. Can you imagine trying to rate the EQ? It's such a personal experience, the answers would take you from heaven to hell.

"Tell us, Mr. And Ms. America, how good was it?"

_____ It was so good, I looked up when it was over and Olympic judges were holding up 6.9s.

_____ Feeling that good is illegal in six Southern states and Wyoming.

_____ It was so good it took the polish off my nails.

_____ It was so good I was speaking in tongues.

_____ The phrase "she's not dead, she's American" comes to mind.

———— I don't know. I fell asleep.

———— The Red Cross is sending in a disaster team.

Despite the aforementioned statistics on frequency of fun, Americans prefer a different kind of action. The survey shows 57 percent of women would skip the sex in favor of going on an unlimited shopping spree with someone else's credit card. And men, those enemies of comparison pricing and dressing room odysseys, those impatient traitors on sale day—42 percent of them would rather go shopping than have sex. Now, what is *that* about, and why doesn't it surface during after-Christmas sales when we could use two extra arms to carry half-off china, and a little more muscle getting to the cash register?

Shopping aside, most Americans would rather make love than ride on the next space shuttle (a pity, since their tax money already has paid for the ticket), and 50 percent would prefer a roll in the hay to being President of the United States for a day. Of course we now know, better than ever, that one does not have to choose between being President and rolling in the White House hay.

Then the survey addressed physical attributes. Men seemed to be more satisfied with themselves and their partners. Seventy-one percent said they were happy with the size of their partner's breasts, which must be why girlie magazines just never sell, and 73 percent were pleased with the size of their own appendages. Only 57 percent of women were happy with their breasts and 58 percent were satisfied with the size of their partner's sexual organ. Somebody is fibbing.

When it comes to actually doing something about it, of the men, 20 percent would choose breast augmentation for their partner and 18 percent would let a surgeon have a go at their own privates. Nineteen percent of women would have breast surgery, but only 10 percent said they would want their man's organ enlarged.

Both sexes seem to agree, it isn't what you've got, it's what you do with it. I was asked to write on the subject for a *Playboy* newsstand special on body language. Why, you ask? Well, it has been written that there is a "restless physicality" to my anchoring on CNN Headline News. I presume that has nothing to do with the antsy feeling I get twice an hour as I approach the sports report, which is the only time I can devote an entire four minutes to running to the ladies' room. In fact, I hold the record for the Headline News One-Way Dash from the Anchor Set to the John in 3-Inch Stilettos (Women's Division): 30 seconds.

Anyway, it is because of this "restless physicality" that *Playboy* wanted this journalist who paints pictures with words through twelve newscasts an evening, to share her thoughts on a more basic—the *most* basic—of human communications skills, body language. As children, we feel free to move in any way we please; unfortunately as we grow into women, we don't dare to do some of the most natural things, like sit with our legs apart if we're wearing a skirt, or thrust out our chests the way men do in order to act assertive or to make a point. Just watch a little girl moving around for five minutes, and she'll deliver a long list of her emotions and thoughts, without saying a word. Then spend five minutes watching a woman. The message still is there, it's just delivered in a more subtle way. And because of that, it can come down on a man like a hammer because he doesn't expect it.

In a business meeting when we're feeling very relaxed and open, we may cross our legs to make Emily Post happy (nobody ever accused her of having too much fun, by the way), but we may find ourselves leaning a bit one way or the other toward the person who is attracting our attention.

Speaking of attention, there is that "I'm listening to every word you're saying" look that seems to take men by surprise. Perhaps they don't get enough of it and aren't used to it. It isn't calculated, really, it's just something we do when we really are interested in what a man is telling us. It has nothing to do with sex, but often it's interpreted that way, so we allow ourselves to be that attentive at our own risk.

Every part of a woman is saying something. Our eyes: They can kill a man, or soothe him. They can seduce him swiftly, or make him relish the challenge of doing all that work himself. We do like it when men wonder what we're thinking. Hell, sometimes we don't know ourselves, but we sure enjoy watching them trying to figure it out. I ask the men, bless their hearts, who are reading this: Ever had a woman look at you over her shoulder, and hold you for just a moment with her eyes? I've seen men stumble when this happens, and it's wonderful fun watching the sheepish looks on their faces when they try to recover.

Of all the demeanors a woman may assume, the most underrated and seductive is "sultry." This is something that comes naturally and can not be faked. The classic example of sultry is the poster for the movie *The Outlaw,* starring my dear friend—and probable cousin—Jane Russell. And she does it with her clothes on. (I am endlessly flattered that I am asked constantly if Jane and I are related. The New York Public Library even called CNN to inquire. A man once suggested to me—and I took it as a tremendous compliment—that Jane and I resemble each other and must be family. "Our eyes?" I asked, "our lips?" "Yeah, right, your eyes," he said. I knew what he meant, I just wanted to hear him say it. An attribute is an attribute, and I'll take one any way I can get it. Being well-endowed may be hell on my seamstress, but it does come with benefits. I never have to wait in line at the Dairy Queen.) What Jane does in that poster pose—now *that's* reclining. And it came to me a couple of years ago that this sort of thing comes naturally, or it doesn't come at all. When Jane and I were sitting at the American Cinema Awards dinner in Los Angeles, and she had to turn her chair around to see the stage, the magic happened again. Other women slumped against the back of their chairs; some sat perkily on the edge. Jane occupied her chair like the German army marching under the Arc de Triomphe, using it as a tool, a prop. She sat at an angle and put an elbow on our table behind her, and leaned back ever so slowly, proving once again that age is a number, and if you've got it, you've got it. Sultry. Seductive. Unbelievable. Now, I keep looking for excuses to lean back. It ain't Jane Russell, but it works.

Let's talk about that little dance we do when we get out of the car. I have given up pantyhose and tights, in favor of sheer, lace-top stockings and garter belts. And for fashion's sake, I make a special effort when I'm in Paris to stock up on opaque black stockings that stay up by themselves. It's so much fun just putting them on in front of the baroque mirrors in my boudoir, I need a cigarette afterward, and I don't even smoke. Half the fun of wearing these things is the enjoyment we get out of it, ourselves. The other half is sharing it with the world. In France, it is not a sin to allow—even plan—for the exposure of a little lace or stocking top when a woman moves; but I believe people are people, and fun is fun wherever you go. If we don't start loosening up a bit in this U.S. of A., we're going to miss a lot. Let me tell you what happened to me today. I just bought a fantastic, bright red Jeep Grand Cherokee, which is higher off the ground than my old BMW, and requires a little more planning for graceful exiting, for people who care. Clearly, for me, that is not a priority. When I arrived at work today I realized, after I had wiggled out of the car in the parking lot, my arms laden with keys, cosmetic bags, newspapers, and other journalistic tools of the trade, that I had inadvertently put on a little show, with my skirt up somewhere around my pelvis. If this had been a pantyhose scenario, nobody would have looked twice. But I was wearing my favorite sheer, black lace-top thigh-highs, and half the parking lot was watching (it was shift change time, and we don't get out much at CNN, so little things make us giggle out of context). Would I have done that on purpose? *Moi?* We all had a laugh! It was light-hearted fun, and frankly, I won't mind if it happens again. *Feminine freedom of body movement*: it would be in the Bill of Rights, if women had written it.

While we're talking about seductive body parts, let's do

something called "The Mouth: Its Other Uses." In the movie *French Kiss*, Meg Ryan's character asks Kevin Kline's character, who is French, about the pout that European women affect when they're talking with their men. What's that all about? He explains that it's a very useful lip movement, which women can use to their best advantage. French females tend to do it more than Americans. I've asked if they manufacture it or if it's natural, and they just look at me with a twinkle in their eyes and say, *"Bien sur,"* of course! It doesn't mean yes, and it doesn't mean no. It means "maybe," and sir, that is the most dangerous answer of all. Use the pout with a lowered head and eyes that look languidly up at the victim, and it's all over. A man might as well pack it in, he's down for the count. And he loves it.

Then there are the inadvertent moves two women make together. Heterosexual women who are comfortable with their bodies and sure of their sexuality have no trouble walking down the street arm in arm. In fact, I challenge American women to try it. These women don't find close contact (hang on, I just spilled Grand Marnier on my computer) in a crowded bar on a Friday night a problem. Again, the effect on men is amazing. I have a very dear girlfriend, Renate, who is German and who owns the popular European-style establishment, Cafe Intermezzo/Dunwoody in Atlanta. On a Friday night we can be found laughing and clicking our champagne glasses, giggling like schoolgirls, and constantly being amused at the absolutely intrigued way men react when we happen to lean against each other, sharing an innocent, intimate moment. Sometimes one of us will lean in and whisper something delightfully mischievous about a man who has just walked in. Other times we'll adjust each other's clothing, as if we're at a slumber party and have found a better way to do it. And we wonder: What are the men thinking? What are they imagining?

When a woman looks at a man and throws her head back, what is she saying? I love watching people, watching men and women interact. And I think that when a woman laughs and exposes the *front* of her neck to a man, she is inviting him to make what he will of the situation. She is opening herself to him, allowing him to make the next move. He can play or he can be serious. Just as long as he understands that she is testing him: He must react some-how. My suggestion is that he reach over and slowly but firmly wrap his hand around the *back* of her neck. After that, he can kiss her or melt her with his eyes—just don't talk for a minute. Then withdraw the hand slowly, lean back and smile. And if that kiss should happen to be on that neck that she offered him, forget about it!

Today, when a woman stands with her waist stretched and her rear end exaggerated, she is not trying to tell the world that she is a recent graduate of the Barbizon School of Modeling. She is sending a message, and it is exactly what you think it is. She is proud of her body, and would like a man to appreciate it, too. And she wouldn't mind if he tried to imagine the matching undies and expensive lingerie she is wearing under-neath. That's the other half of the fun, remember? You might even be able to see traces of the lace, or you might make note of the fact that under that poured-on body suit, there is no sign of a panty line, which is a clear indication she didn't miss the Victoria's Secret silk thong sale.

Something few people address when they're talking about body language is breathing. There are moments when the woman who is interested in a man will actually hold her breath as she anticipates what will happen. Maybe he just appeared in front of her and she is taken by surprise, or he has poured her a nice Cabernet Sauvignon and is looking deeply into her eyes as he makes no move to give her the glass, or she has just caught him watching her as she slipped on her new silk robe. It is a moment full of promise, and it can tell him everything.

Because I'm on camera so much, I am very used to controlling my hand movements—so much so, that in my free time I don't use them the way I would if I were, say, a bubble dancer. I don't rest my arm on my elbow when I talk, with my hand flopping around and one finger sticking lazily out. Someone might think it's a comment on the story I'm reading. And we all might like it too much. But along with being a player in this body language game, I'm also an observer, and it's interesting to see how other women use their hands. Some let them lie wherever they land, whether that space is their lap or somebody else's. I've seen women whose fingers seem to have gotten stuck on the top of their breasts, as they idly contemplate something that amuses them, or maybe they're just appreciating the fabric. This, also, has been known to drive a man nuts, especially if it happens during a staff meeting. Which brings to mind a woman I know who is in the habit of sucking on the end of her index finger when she does math. She's an accountant. She has a large clientele.

There are other things a woman does with her hands when she's concentrating and some of them are legal, like playing with her hair. If it's long, she can wind it around her fingers and there's a lot of action: a little caress here, a little curl there, pulling this, tugging and stretching that, and before you know it she has created—perhaps quite innocently—that unstudied, post-coital look guaranteed to send male imaginations spinning out of control.

And now, I have saved the best for last. The female of the species has the option of unleashing the Ultimate Secret Weapon that is so subtle yet so powerful that it is the most lethal of all mating calls, when executed properly. This one is performed in one smooth motion, and it is never an accident: She raises her arm, running her slightly separated fingers up the side of her neck, elbow high and out, raising and showing off the line of her breast, head back. Her hand continues its ever-so-slow journey up the nape of her neck as the fingers separate and "comb" through her hair all the way to the ends. A man watches this smoldering, universal message and wonders if there is some mistake. There isn't. And if she should happen to arch her back during this maneuver, he'll swear his shoes are on fire.

The body is a beautiful thing. Body language is what makes the world go 'round.

Things We Hope Men Never Figure Out and Things We'd Pay Money for Men to Figure Out

The psychology of physical attraction is a wonderful thing. And we are happy to share our thoughts with the opposite sex when they want to listen. But there are things we hope men never figure out. I hesitate to discuss this first topic, because it's giving away so much. My friends, in fact, are offering me bribes to leave it out. They haven't gone so far as to call me a traitor to my gender, but I know that's next. Still, it's critical to the integrity of this chapter, and by the time this book is in the hands of the other side, we will have come up with a more sophisticated weapon. The all-important entry is:

Caller ID

A tool so useful in assessing where a man is coming from, it's almost a sexual aid. It's as good a gauge of a man's testosterone level as you will find. It typically stores at least eighty phone numbers with time and date, which means a woman is able to determine who has called, how often, and from where—

provided the caller didn't have his number blocked, as many women do for their own protection. Then you have to wonder why a guy would do that.

You say you've been trying to call? I know you haven't, because your number's not on the Caller ID, and it would've been nice to know you at least were thinking of me. You say you called, but not from your own phone? *Nobody's* number is on the Caller ID. Now there's Call Waiting ID so you can see that the man you dated last week and really liked is trying to get through to you, while you're wasting your time on the line with Satan's son. You can tell, before you interrupt your conversation, who's on the other end. Still, I've stopped paying much attention to it, throwing a cloth over the unit because the damned blinking light makes me crazy.

We Can Read Their Minds

We may not get all the elements in the right order all the time, but we come damn close. And so, we can tell when they're lying, even if we're not exactly sure about the specifics.

$20 Worth of Roses

. . . and the "L" word can fix almost anything they've done or have not done. We know better, but we can't help ourselves. Flowers speak to our souls; "I love you" speaks to every body part. Men who have great difficulty saying it under normal circumstances report favorable results when they unleash it as a last resort.

When a Man Tells You Something Negative About Himself, You Can Take It to the Bank

I can't count the times I've heard women saying, "Now, dear, I'm sure that's not true. You're not giving yourself enough credit. You're being too hard on yourself. You're too critical of yourself and you're overestimating what you think are your shortcomings, just so I won't be disappointed."

Please. If he tells you, "I'm a slob," believe him. You'll be picking up after him till you can't stand it anymore, till you want to take all the dirty socks and Jockey shorts that are piled in the corner and tie them together and strangle him in his sleep. If he tells you, "I'm a bastard," for God's sake believe him. He knows himself better than you do. If you don't listen, you'll awaken one night to strange noises in the living room and find "sweetheart" debriefing the baby-sitter he was supposed to have taken home an hour ago, while they finish off the bottle of expensive wine you and he opened that afternoon.

Men somehow feel they can tell us these things, because we care so much that we'll ignore them. This allows them to feel cleansed, absolved of whatever they might do, since they have confessed in advance. And, should the subject come up months

or years later, they can honestly say, "I *told* you I was a bastard/
slob/pyromaniac/keyhole molester. You should have listened
to me!" But we do ignore the warnings, because we just love
being in love. Which is one of the most endearing things about
us—and one of the most threatening to our well-being.

Sometimes It's Good They Don't Listen

"Sweetheart, chewing tobacco really doesn't help a man's
image."

A week later:

"I don't think you understand. Chewing tobacco, whether
you think I know you're doing it or not, is a romance killer.
Capice?"

Another week later:

"Now we have two problems. Either you aren't listening to
what I'm telling you, or you're listening and are doing it anyway. I *know* you're doing it, and the picture in my head dis-
gusts me."

A month later:

"Honey, I reached down between the seat on the driver's
side of the car and the console to pick up my earring, and do
you know what I came up with? A big, ole, moist wad of
tobacco. This is not good. Are you hearing me?"

Three more weeks:

"Yes, I *do* have a headache tonight, and I'm going to have
one *every* night until I stop hearing you spitting tobacco juice

into the goddamn toilet, do you *understand,* because you're making me *crazy!*"

At this point, you should be writing him a thank-you note on your best stationery, because he has alerted you to the fact that he has the cooperative spirit of a stone, and it isn't going to get any better. The tobacco is not the problem, it is a symptom. The problem is that you have an uncooperative man who really doesn't take you seriously and doesn't care what you think. Start packing. In this case, he did you a favor by ignoring you.

Most Things Aren't Forever, but Sometimes They're for Long Enough

If we can do it, IF we can do it, we can use this philosophy, this fact, to our advantage in just about every area of life. As it applies to men, it is an indispensable adage. How often have you anguished over the end of a relationship, wondering if you should have handled something differently, imagining other outcomes to the same scenario, all of it based upon *your* doing something differently?

Take one of those scenarios, maybe the end of your marriage or engagement, and look at it with the thought that it lasted as long as it was *supposed* to. Consider that nothing you could have done—short of selling out the things you believe in—could have saved it. Imagine that your life is a series of scenarios, a rotogravure of little stories about you and the men who pass through. Be honest enough with yourself to see that you were being you, and that's all you can be. To extend the length of those relationships you would have had to be someone else, and to have done that, you would have had to sacrifice a little bit more of who you are, each time. This is not to say that these relationships were bad. You learned something from each one. And—even for a brief time—there was something good about them, something that contributed to who you are today. If you are going with this thought, you will appreciate a little thing that has "said it all" for me, for years. Edna St. Vincent Millay wrote:

Well, I have lost you; and I lost you fairly;
In my own way, and with my full consent.
Say what you will, kings in a tumbrel rarely
Went to their deaths more proud than this one went.
Some nights of apprehension and hot weeping
I will confess; but that's permitted me;
Day dried my eyes; I was not one for keeping
Rubbed in a cage a wing that would be free.
If I had loved you less or played you slyly
I might have held you for a summer more,
But at the cost of words I value highly,
And no such summer as the one before.
Should I outlive this anguish—and men do—
I shall have only good to say of you.

A level-headed approach to love. But remember, she also wrote:

My candle burns at both ends;
    It will not last the night;
But ah, my foes, and oh, my friends—
    It gives a lovely light!

What the hell.

What You Start With Is What You End Up With

My friend Valerie's mother, Evelyn, offered this wise advice to her teenage daughter, and Valerie is fond of repeating it to me whenever I get out of line—whenever I find I'm the only one doing the worrying/explaining/hand-holding/understanding. You may think you can get along just fine shouldering the emotional load, always being the one to initiate those intimate little displays of affection that you love so much, the ones that make you feel all warm and protected, and make him feel so appreciated. Then one day, you realize the load is pure, Grade A, Colorado bull product, and you're tired of having to wear boots every time you go in the house, but you don't know how to change it.

Avoid this nasty predicament by working that stuff out from the very beginning. It has been suggested that living together before marriage enables you to smooth out the rough edges, if you take advantage of the opportunity. So do it in a classy way. "Hey, Homer, I know how much you love watching the tractor pull, but if you could drag yourself away from the television long enough to gimme a little goodnight kiss, now that I'm going off to fifteen hours of janitorial work at the hazardous compounds section of the germ-warfare plant, I'd sure appreciate it, sweetie. Mmmm . . . Ya *know* how ah *luv* ya." Or, to the man who showers with the curtain open despite your repeated, softly spoken pleas for compliance, and leaves half an inch of water on the bathroom floor, perhaps pin a little note to the curtain: "Here in the West Wing of the White House, the staff frowns on violations of bathroom protocol, and considers improper shower etiquette grounds for denial of special privileges. In other words, keep the goddamn water off the floor, or sleep in the living room tonight!"

Everything a Man Thinks and Does Is Related to Two Things: Sex and Money

You already knew this.

Choosing a Man Is Like Picking a Dessert

Sometimes it's best just to go with the one who appeals to you at first glance. You'll find out all about the calories whether you want to or not. But by all means, go with something that looks good.

1. Do judge a book by its cover. We don't have time to

send in a team of experts. This isn't a UN mission, here.

2. Beware. Don't be foolish about obvious signs. If you've got a defective one on the line, remember it's not stamped on his forehead, "Hey, I'm a mental case."

Maybe we could come up with some sort of infrared forehead code that shows up only under a special light that women carry in their purses:

MC: mental case

PL: phalically challenged

M: married

M+: married with ex-wife who rides a broom

PL: professional liar

UI: under indictment

BS: bisexual (BS has unlimited uses as you might imagine, but we're going with bisexual, since nothing will kill a relationship faster than introducing your boyfriend to your gay brother at the Fourth of July parade and finding out that not all the tailgating is going on in the traffic.)

LQ: this guy has an "IQ lower than his tire pressure"

I: indecisive

B: look up "boring" in the dictionary and you find his picture

Even a Good-Looking Dessert Has to Offer Something Special

My friend Renate's mother offered this clever little German addage, "You can't eat from an empty plate, no matter how attractive it is." If he's absolutely gorgeous but there's nothing going on upstairs, you're going to get awfully tired trying to amuse yourself on a Saturday night watching this guy buff his nails.

The Man You're Stuck on Is Not the Only Dessert in Town

Men and women are the same all over the world. Men are men, and women are pissed off. There's a German song that must have an equivalent in every language. It says, "Why cry when a man leaves you, when there's another one just around the corner?"

We Know Men Want Us to Be the Bad Guy

Why is it that if it's something bad, they want us to say it first? We both can know that we have no future together, that our last date was from hell, that our ox is in a ditch. But the *woman* has to be the one to say it.

"Last night was a mistake."

"Last YEAR was a mistake."

Having said it, why do we have to listen to the inevitable, "What do you mean by that?" You know what I mean by that! We can't stop arguing long enough to have fun. There is something seriously wrong when we can't even share intimate moments without arguing over whose fault it is that Thumper didn't visit Sleeping Beauty last night. Why do *I* have to be the one to bring it on home? It isn't fair that women have to be the first ones to say the obvious. Notice that if it's good news, men can't deliver it fast enough.

Then, there are the . . . Things We Would Pay Money for Men to Figure Out.

Leave a Message!

Men think simply dialing our phone numbers, whether they make contact or not, fulfills their obligation; and we are supposed to know, through some sixth sense, that they let the phone ring.

I used to console myself with the knowledge that I could see on the Caller ID that he at least had tried, until I realized he had no idea I knew. So then I made the little rule that if he left no message, he had not called. Period. Common sense has to begin somewhere; I hope you can see that this entire dilemma elevates the classic "male-female communication" debate to a frightening new level when we realize that there is miscommunication even before we open our mouths.

Pay Attention

We beg men to believe that when we discuss our relationships with them in terms of its length and potential, we're exploring all the aspects. To us, it's about "You and Me," and nothing else. If his mind wanders, there could be trouble. It's not about the 49ers season stats, or tee time on Saturday.

We Want Them to Understand

. . . the reasons we feel the way we do about virtually everything. We want them to, because we figure that if they understand, they can't help but agree. And we love it so when they agree.

How to Turn On the Dishwasher

Perhaps if they pretended it's a new 50-inch, high-definition television set with SurroundSound and a voice-activated remote control, on Superbowl Sunday, they could do it. Or they could imagine it's something they pulled off the black box they got from Buddy at work, who promised videos of Finnish girls doing things they never saw before. Or one of those fancy new steering wheels with the cruise control buttons, all six of them, on the front, and buttons for controlling the CD player, the tape player, and the radio on the back. Men can learn how to operate these things in the first sixty seconds they're in the car; but pouring the detergent into the dishwasher, locking the door, and turning the knob remain a mystery to them, the sort of mystery they approach with only mild interest and no desire to solve.

The Three Most Important Words

They used to be "I love you," but women now agree that all of us are questioning the very definition of love. Some of us even are insisting that the L word not be used, in favor of more descriptive verbiage. The three most important words now are the ones that suggest a genuine willingness to assess a woman's state of well-being *and do something about it*: "Did you come?"

Stonewalling Is for Masons

From a recent study that's been making the E-mail rounds because it's so true: the conversational maneuver known as stonewalling on the part of the male is an indicator, if not a cause, of a serious breakdown in the relationship. To stonewall is to shut off communication with the person who is trying to have a discussion with you. For our purposes here, it means a man who gives no acknowledgment at all that the woman who is addressing him is getting a message through, or even that he is awake and in a receiving mode.

Déjà vu? For the longest time, I found the only way to carry on a conversation with a certain male was to get face-to-face with him and jump in with words as soon as he accidentally made eye contact. If men stonewall with skill, it can put us off for weeks and it works quite well. This particular man risked whiplash when he faked a last-second maneuver to move away and refocus on a far wall, a sort of Hail Mary Pass-you-by; but my coming in close was his undoing. Unfortunately, it still didn't mean that he had to move his lips in anything resembling an answer.

If only men would understand that three minutes of direct conversation, even if it ends in "Go to hell, and take your goddamn Bergdorf card with you!" are worth twenty agonizing minutes of trying to establish contact. Which brings us to . . .

Men Turn Us into Perry Mason's Understudy, and We Don't Like It

The men in our lives have forced us to become people we don't like—women who have to do all the asking, all the deduction, all the mental gymnastics—to get one complete answer. It can take weeks. Months. We feel and sound like the trial attorneys we never wanted to be when we have to return again and again to the same subject to get a feel for what's really going on. "Why is she still calling you? Are you giving her hope? Does

she know it's over? Have you specifically *told* her? But it's been three months, why not? Are you not sure about it? Of course I trust you, it's just that this has been going on and on, and I'm a little concerned. No, I am *not* giving you the third degree, I'm just asking questions in hopes of finding out the tiniest, fucking thing about what's going on with my life. And don't *ever* say again that I'm just like her—that selfish, slovenly *bitch*—when I'm just trying to have a simple conversation with you, the man I love! *No, I am NOT through! My God, do you hear me? I'm SHOUTING! I am not Kreskin, goddamn it, I can't read your mind, and I need to TALK to you! I need for YOU to TALK TO ME!"*

We all have been through this. It happens partly because the men aren't keeping us up-to-date, and partly because *they* have no idea what's going on, since (escape artists that they are) they never get around to analyzing it/forcing the issue/ telling the old girlfriend it's over/breaking the bad news, as- suming (correctly) that the women in their past and present will do all the work. Every woman I've interviewed for this book who has been involved with a man who still has one foot in another relationship says the same thing. It's like going with a centipede and waiting for the other shoe to drop. And it will drive you out of your mind.

Pay for the Damn Drinks, It's Worth It

He may decide that since he knows he isn't going to score tonight, he won't waste his money on paying for the lady's

drink after he has invited himself over to her table. But here's the news flash: he could run into her again, at the same meat market or another one. If he sprang for the eight bucks the first time, he'd have *such* a good chance of striking pay dirt the next time, instead of a snowball's chance in hell. He really can't afford *not* to pay. He should consider it an investment. The corollary to this belongs in the segment on Things We Hope Men Never Figure Out, and that is that if he doesn't think she's worth the price of a martini, he's doing her a big favor by *not* covering the tab. She can see quite clearly that he's a shortsighted guy who would make the perfect chess opponent or houseboy.

A Present Is Not a Promise, but It's a Helluva Statement

It shouts that he is thinking of her, that he has put some effort into picking out something that suits her. She will appreciate the smallest token, because it comes from the heart. If it happens to be jewelry, however inexpensive, then she has something that warms to her skin and something she can touch, to remind her of him. If it should be beautiful lingerie, an interesting thing happens. When they've had a fight, she actually can find some comfort in wearing it close to her body. Women are funny, unpredictable and sentimental, and that's why men are fascinated with us beyond the initial "Lay down baby, I think I love ya."

A General "I'm Sorry" Works Only on *I Dream of Jeannie*

"I'm sorry" is way too successful a phrase for men. We accept it as the apology, the peace we're hoping for, reasoning that words don't come easily to them. We don't stop to think that they have no trouble relating the attributes of their favorite car, or last season's Atlanta Braves stats, or stock quotes.

Perhaps they truly do become inarticulate with us. So, if they can't find the words, we ought to help them out. Instead of an apology taking half the day, I suggest coming up with a multiple-choice form. Keep copies all over the house and even in the car, with possibly a few purse-size versions for those awkward moments when you want to salvage the evening out. The man in your life can simply check off the offenses that apply, or check "other" and write in his own. For this, allow twenty extra minutes.

I'M SORRY FOR:
_____ BEING LATE
_____ FORGETTING YOUR BIRTHDAY
_____ REMEMBERING YOUR BIRTHDAY (YOU STILL LOOK 25)
_____ FORGETTING OUR ANNIVERSARY
_____ LETTING MY SECRETARY CHOOSE YOUR GIFT
_____ AND TELLING HER TO ORDER ONE FOR HERSELF

____ NOT CALLING

____ CALLING

____ NOT KNOWING WHAT I DID WRONG

____ NOT CARING WHAT I DID WRONG

____ EVERY OFFENSE I'VE COMMITTED SINCE NOON

____ OTHER:_____

With this handy form, your beloved can simply check off the ones he chooses, like ordering a pizza or having the oil changed and the tires rotated.

Relationships are nothing if not challenging and entertaining. And I have found there are benefits and drawbacks to all of them, including the ones I don't even know I have, with total strangers. People who watch me on television. So let's have some fun now with viewer mail.

Viewer Mail

Can we talk about the kind of mail a female network news anchor *really* gets? I could discuss this with another anchor, but it's more fun to scare the bejesus out of a stranger.

When you're on the tube all over the world, in 170 countries, your recognition factor is sky-high. People everywhere see you every day, whether they like it or not: in bars, at home, at the airport, everywhere but public bathrooms and that's probably next. From the students who hang out on the Charles Bridge in Prague, to the better-to-do entrepreneurial residents of the newest fertile-market territory, Vietnam, expatriates tune to CNN Headline News to see what they're missing (or not missing) back home. They're all watching. You're featured in magazines and newspapers, and even on other people's television shows. If you're the sort of person who finds it easy to believe her own PR, this kind of exposure can be a real head trip. Me, I wish I had the sort of ego that could take advantage of it. Like demanding only silver M & M's in a Tiffany bowl in my office, where chilled Moët et Chandon and Rocky, my massage therapist, are ready at the end of each grueling half hour of reporting the news. With twelve half hours in an evening, I'd be very relaxed and very looped by the time I left work, making for some amazing news copy. Then, of course, the limo would whisk me home.

While that lovely fairy tale is not the case, I admit I do find the public attention very flattering, and it has worked to my advantage. It worked in Budapest during one of those ill-advised, miserable winter sightseeing trips when I just didn't take anybody's advice and jumped a train from Vienna for the four-hour ride into one of the bleakest scenes ever to burn itself into my memory. I had not made a hotel reservation, because back then I thought it was more fun to just "hang out" and take what came along, all in the spirit of adventure. On this occasion I found that having a familiar face that smiled out at the folks from their very rare, very old little TV sets, made all the difference in getting a room at a sold-out hotel on a frozen, gray December evening . . . back in those nasty Hungarian Commie days when they came down hard on visitors who weren't tucked obediently into their barn floorlike little beds in clumsily bugged, '60s era guest rooms by midnight. The only alternative would have been to roam the train station all night, dodging armed guys wearing funny little green hats with red stars on them.

On another occasion, I was especially grateful for my dubious reputation. It was in Atlanta, where a tractor-trailer accident had brought traffic to an absolute halt. After four hours in the car trying to get to work by airtime, I joined other drivers in going a little nuts. My Deepak Chopra–inspired cool dissolved into wild beating on the steering wheel and fretful, uncontrolled sobbing as if Victoria's Secret had just closed its last store. Then, through a sea of red taillights and office buildings, I caught sight of my destination, my Bali Hai: a tower of CNN Center. This was at 7:20 P.M., twenty minutes after I would have begun my first newscast. A little voice in my head told me that if ever there was a time to whip onto the shoulder of the road and make a run for it, this was it. So, with a renewed sense of purpose, I made my move. Forty-five seconds later, *a cop stopped me cold.* Now in a towering rage and certain of a $200 citation, I flew out of the car, slammed the door, and bellowed that I just wanted "to get to*@!# work!" Well, my friend, let me tell you it was a near-religious experience when the officer, who knew me from the news and must have figured too many White House stories had given me brain rot, made no effort to give me a ticket, but kept his distance, astonished at my behavior and observing me as if I were behind glass. He waited until I wound down, and finally said, *"Lynne, what in the world are you doing?"*

Public recognition also means that viewers I haven't met yet want to communicate. After all, they say we've known each other for years, and we've shared so much. In the evenings, as I'm doing a story on the fighting in Bosnia, some couple out there—maybe you and the spouse—are sharing an intimate, end-of-day moment with the American Express bill. I deliver a story about the presidential debates, and you remember to reheat the Sunday chicken. We roll video of a busload of dancing girls from Sistersville, West Virginia, and you go back to the kitchen for the corn.

With such a rich history of sharing between us, viewers want to write. That's nice. Or call. Also nice. We probably won't actually talk, but it's the thought that counts. Or maybe they'll send a little something more, in a parcel. We'll get back to that in a minute.

About those letters: It isn't that I don't appreciate the effort. It's just better if they aren't so gross that I have to wear surgical gloves to look at them. And, since I don't see every bit of the mail that comes in, viewers ought not stay up nights with the Crayolas, writing me creatively illustrated tales of self-love in front of the TV set. They certainly shouldn't explain to me how the federal government has conspired to control their thoughts by implanting a mysterious piece of metal in their pelvic area. The word from our security people, who do read all the mail, is that somebody has beat them to it, and anyway the government isn't that smart.

In my sixteen years with CNN, I have heard from them all: from choirboys and con artists, prisoners and paranoids, and the sanest people on the planet to those in danger of visiting another planet . . . very soon. They are the most fun, because they haven't gone round the bend yet, and if they keep writing, you can watch it happen. Sure, there are the colorful stalkers and perverts, but they aren't really *fun*. They're just the sort of aggravation that keeps the legal system going.

I have developed a few standard rules that I follow in opening fan mail, which I thought I would share with you:

- *First, Examine the Envelope.* Look at the return address. If there's a long number after his name, he may not be available for a while, but there's always the chance he's in the tank for more than tearing the tags off pillows.

I shoot that one straight to Security. If the writing is really big or really small, or it's so rhythmically precise that it makes your eyes cross, this may be the sort of person who has a pathological fascination with lining up the bathroom towels and avoiding sidewalk cracks. This one gets his own file. If the envelope reeks of aftershave, especially if it has that sweet, roach-spray bouquet, there's definitely no autographed picture going out.

- *Always Use a Letter Opener.* I have discovered that if I don't, I can find myself in the john scrubbing my hands raw after I read some guy's description of his unique relationship with his pit bull, and I realize that I handled the part of the envelope he licked. His dog, it turns out, also is a fan. A really big fan.

- *Once Inside the Envelope, Watch for Falling Objects.* A hard hat wouldn't be a bad idea. On one occasion, just as I was removing a pungent little herb-and-feather "good luck charm" from the envelope, a ceiling tile came crashing down on my head. Another time, I was showered with sand from Desert Storm, which the writer was kind enough to point out was tainted with a biological weapon. Obviously he didn't realize that if I got sick too, I wouldn't be around to tell his side of the story. But when you're being that clever, logic can wait.

Some of the most interesting things to fall out of envelopes have been photographs, collages of my head glued on every sort of body, gender-be-damned. Although I'm especially fond of a combination of me with short hair (a Polaroid taken off the TV screen) on a well-oiled male weight-lifter's frame, I am bitterly disappointed that no one has me in the image of my heroine: Xena, Warrior Princess. Other pictures are viewer photographs you could describe only as mugshots. One in particular has become a newsroom favorite: a guy holding a big fish he caught. They do rather resemble each other. The fish is the one without the hat.

These few lines from recent mail will give you a feel for the kind of stuff that makes its way through sleet, snow, and dark of night to wind up one bright day in the mailroom of the network. I never have met any of these writers:

- "Dear Lynne, I'd love to wrap my feet around your nice long hair. I hope our Good Lord has helped you in your time of need." He has. I have your address and social security number.
- "Lynn, here's the plan. Wear a silk blouse, no bra, and turn the temp in the studio down to sixty."
- "Attn. Miss Lynne Russell, Headline News, The whole world is under the control of the evil one." Really? I had no idea my ex-husband's first wife had it in her.
- "Dear Ms. Russell, This sounds silly, but as I trace the outline of your hair with my eyes and wonder about you, your interests, and the kind of woman you are, I ask myself what kind of fool am I to write you."
- "Dear Lynne, I am God, do my will! Please send me a plane ticket so I can come there and work, and the

name of a hotel there that I can stay in, and tell me about the job I will be doing there." Hello, Security?

- "To Lynn Russell, The impression I get from you is that you wanted to meet me. I'm real boring, I don't talk much, but I like fishing." Wow.

- On a Valentine: "I know we'll be together one day soon. All my love forever, David. XOXO."

- "My wife's birthday is coming up soon and I was wondering if you could send her an autographed photo. It would mean so much to her." What a great compliment!

- On a postcard that followed an absolutely blank postcard: "You know that request? That wasn't fair, I'll say it to anyone because I do."

- "Dear Lynne, If you were at a charity fair selling kisses at $100 a pop, I'd mortgage my house." I love a man with priorities.

And now, to those parcels. Just pretend you're going through airport security, and you'll know how a package coming into CNN feels:

- First comes our pal the X ray. I say, go over that sucker till it *glows*. Security won't tell everything that has been picked up this way, but I remember hearing a $40,000 Rolex was exploded in the parking lot. (Just kidding. It could've been $20,000.) Door keys also show up on X ray—as in the neat little packet containing a guy's apartment keys, a black nightie, and a long list of the hockey games we were going to watch. I'm sorry I missed that one.

- If the parcel passes the X-ray test, but I just don't have a good feeling about it, I let *my friend Terry's hound dog* have a go at it. This dog can sniff out two important things: dead or near-dead anything, and chocolate. If the dog does not sit and beg, it is not chocolate. At this point, it does no harm to . . .
- Poke around inside with a cattle prod. We've had no accidents, here. As we say in the business: no arrests, no injuries.
- If by now the package appears innocent, *open with care.* And I'll tell you why. *Cash,* a girl's best friend. Not always big bills, but it's cash all the same—and it can be a mixed blessing. For instance, a good-size stack of $2 bills, with the name and social security number of the sender, and a cute little political message, scrawled on each one. Still legal tender, but I couldn't *give* them away in the newsroom.

At CNN, we do have a policy that on-air people don't accept expensive gifts. They are returned with a nice "thank you" whenever possible, or they are sent to charity. Who, anyway, would send a diamond wedding ring set without enclosing a letter or even his name? It really happened. The package was postmarked "Washington, D.C.," which makes perfect sense—a man with such a thready grip on reality, such a penchant for throwing money away, could only be a lawmaker. This was two years ago, and he's still waiting for an answer, unless his term has expired and the bus to Steubenville has taken him away.

Which brings to mind one last point: Every letter, every package represents a person, an individual. I can feel all warm and fuzzy about some of it, but I can't help but wonder about the rest: How do these people spend their days? Are they law-abiding? Do they hold positions of authority? Are they ripping off 7-Elevens? Are they reproducing?

What about the realtor in Texas who hasn't maxed out his MasterCard, and continues his three-year tradition of sending expensive flower arrangements accompanied by intricate love poems ("Roses Are Red, Violets Are Blue, You Love Me and I Love You"). It's his way of communicating after Security warned him to cease his written suggestions that I was about to leave my then-husband for him, and he could wait no longer. Imagine. This person is driving a car.

And what about the D.C. attorney who was convinced I was talking to him through the TV? Intimate dinners together, reminiscing about old times, and making big plans for long, exotic trips . . . as I watched him undress. With all the "talking" we did, he was the first lawyer who didn't bill me.

You have to maintain your sense of humor about these folks; you really can't let it get to you. My former husband was especially good-natured about this and became quite used to it, although every once in a while he got that *I'm-going-to-take-him-apart* look.

I don't want to leave you with the impression that everyone who writes is certifiable. I have discovered kindness that transcends distance and time; and there is much good in people.

I, myself, never would write a fan letter—perhaps out of fear of making a fool of myself. No smart comments, please. What I do is live TV and it's a living. But I never would send a one-of-a-kind gift, knowing I might never hear a word about it. Yet people do, and they are as unique as the things they send. A man who served in the military during World War II shared a valuable possession: earrings and a bracelet he made from tiny shells he picked up on a Pacific island during a lull in the fighting. Those, I kept. A sense of history is so rare these days, so precious, so elusive. It reminds me that we are a "flicker in eternity," and we really ought to mellow out, because it's all basically the same—only the names, dates, and winners of the conflicts change. A sobering, grounding, and oddly reassuring thought.

There are people who are given to sending things to a total stranger, and keep sending them, without any indication that the intended recipient has even set eyes on them. Like cartons full of snacks and bottled beverages and a collection of unrelated items—from baseball caps and coffee beans to computer wrist supports and children's books—which weigh so much that the cost of UPSing me the package must be more than the cost of the contents. Other gifts are less of a mystery. There was the inmate at the state prison in Moundsville, West Virginia, who hand-made a lovely wooden jewelry box lined with velvet. And the dear woman who sewed an array of lacy little scarves the year I was really into stuffing them in my suit pockets. I did wear a couple of them and I hope it made her happy.

The Baby Boomer's Guerrilla Guide to Middle Age

Age is a number. To encourage you to live this maxim as if it were tattooed on your forehead, I'd like to explain how this point of view, this truth, is taken to heart on a daily basis in other parts of the world. You know, of course, this means we're going back to Paris. Not long ago I went there to think some things through, as I so often have over the years. For some reason my head is clearer there, and naturally there is the added advantage of being geographically unavailable to most kinds of trouble that could find me at home. All you have to do is settle in at a table at a place like the famous Café de la Paix. You could be anywhere in the city; this happens to be the place where this brilliant idea first struggled to the surface of my consciousness—a great place for people-watching, in an upscale part of town on the Right Bank right across from the old Opera. Papa Hemingway also liked to pass the time here and perhaps he's hanging around, prodding writers to become inspired to think past themselves. Immediately you notice that you feel less stressed and more at ease, which is the beginning of not worrying about things you can't change, especially age. It's the perfect vantage point for observing people who obviously feel freer to be so much more themselves, so much less concerned about conforming than we are back home. And as you look at the faces around you, it will strike you that there is a mixture of ages that you are not used to seeing, just hanging out in close proximity to each other—and that is very comforting. They all are doing basically the same things, talking about family and the weather, the next holiday (Europeans are very big on "going on holiday"), those outrageous taxes, and those outrageous politicians.

On one particular evening, I had been trying for an hour to ignore the young lovers at the table to my left as they flirted and kissed. I felt it was an intrusion to watch them. I found it amusing, and tremendously encouraging, that when at last I looked up again from my writing, they had been replaced by a man and a woman with white hair, arm-in-arm, also laughing and giving each other little kisses.

In Europe, there is less emphasis on age, period. They have been able to maintain that "neighborhood of all ages" feeling because of their lifestyle of walking and taking good public transportation, which places the whole lot of them shoulder-to-shoulder out there in the real world. We, on the other hand, have become quite successful at isolating ourselves in little, climate-controlled boxes of steel on wheels. We drive like a bat outta hell to get there, and then sit for ten extra minutes at our destination, staring at the trunk of another steel box with its back-up lights on, waiting for it to leave so we can pull into a parking spot that will enable us to shave fifty feet off our walk into the mall. This way, we can avoid inconvenient contact with strangers, and deprive our lazy butts the opportunity to develop a little healthy muscle mass. To work the muscles, we get back into our little boxes with all the windows closed tight, even on a beautiful day, and drive to a health club where we pay good money to make like a gerbil on somebody's treadmill. We ensure the headphones we are wearing eliminate the sound of natural human chitchat. And God forbid we should make eye contact with someone who is not wearing headphones. There could be real trouble. A conversation.

We never may be able to give ourselves all the perks of the European lifestyle. It isn't our fault—things have gone too far afield—but we can at least see that there is much to be gained by eliminating, or de-emphasizing, the self-imposed isolation that keeps us from spending time around the very young and the old. If we ever are able to do that, we can discover again that age is no big thing.

No matter what I'm telling you, I'd be lying if I didn't admit that I don't need to be reminded of this myself. On this particular trip, I had just arrived on the early flight and my hotel room wasn't ready. So I left my luggage at the hotel and walked to the beautiful Tuileries gardens, which once were part of palace grounds when the adjacent Louvre museum was home to royalty. This was late October. Some of the flowers still were in bloom, which made it seem like summer; and over at the lovely, round pond the man with the pushcart was at his usual station, renting his small boats with colorful, patched sails to children. Maybe they play Nintendo in the evening, but during the day these kids are content to pray for a breeze that will carry the boats to the other side of the pond, where they wait to push them back out with long sticks. It's a lesson in patience, I've tried it myself. I acknowledge that for this American there is the growing, ugly urge, about ten minutes after the breeze dies down, to jump in the water and grab the damn boat and hurl it a good ten feet. Anyway, it had rained and it was reminiscent of summer after a shower, yet the leaves on the trees were turning magnificent golds and oranges, against the wet, dark limbs. I was fatigued from lack of sleep on the flight, and no lack of unsorted thoughts spinning in my brain. As I sat with my head in my hands, hunched over against the surprisingly cold wind, the official Tuileries welcoming committee showed up: pigeons and sparrows, come to see if I'd brought them anything.

I must have looked pretty dejected. A very kind-looking, nicely dressed man appeared and sat beside me and asked if I was all right. I thought, yeah, what a come-on. I told him, *"Oui, mais il faut que je pense tout seul maintenant, merci."* Translation: "Yes, but I need to think all by myself now, thank you." He replied that a garden is a very good place for contemplating the world, and he reassured me that everything would be all right, ending with *"Vous êtes comme une jeune fille avec votre tristesse."* "You're like a little girl with your sadness." I was quite surprised when he kissed me on both cheeks, said he had to get to work, and was gone. If I had been eighty, he would have said the same thing. You see, age really is a number, and this was the reminder I needed. The child is in all of us, and it's easy to see and to feel if we just will let it happen. It's what's inside you and what you do with it that counts. And so we must be gentle with ourselves and with others, regardless of the miles we all have racked up.

Unfortunately this does not work with everyone we encounter, especially if we belong to that segment of the population known as the Baby Boomers. *Some* of us, now in our forties and fifties, are content to settle down and quietly slip over the hill. Then, there are those of us who will do that when hell freezes over or when Larry King stops getting married, whichever comes first, which makes it time for . . .

The Baby Boomer's Guerrilla Guide to Middle Age

And why not? Lots of magazines devote lots of pages to tricky little ways to fool your public if you're twenty-five with a dating crisis, or thirty with an achievement crisis. So it's absolutely fair to talk here about being forty—or fifty—with a public relations crisis. In this wonderful America of ours, it's all image.

And it's all in knowing where you should devote your energy. It's amazing what we can do with makeup, smoke and mirrors. When I took my first television news anchor job, I obviously wanted my appearance to present me and my station in the best possible light. As part of that, I was absolutely positive that my nails had to be meticulously groomed, better than they'd ever been before. The manicure had to be flawless and the color had to be perfect. You can imagine that going out "in the field" and doing reports plays hell with your hands—digging through camera bags for microphones and videotapes, climbing rock formations to be in that interesting shot, and diving into your purse for mosquito spray and hair spray. (Yes, the day I got them mixed up five minutes before a live report is a day they still talk about in whispers at a station in Florida.) Every time I turned around I was touching up the polish and putting on hand cream. I hadn't spent that much time on a body part since my freshman year of college, when . . . anyway, the nails were so perfect it makes me sick to think about it. Six months later, when I was looking at a tape of the show—we call it an air check—a powerful thought elbowed its way past everything I was seeing, a thought that would change my life forever: *you couldn't see my nails at all.* I could have trimmed them with hedge clippers and painted them with a toothbrush, and nobody would have known the difference. That meant, yes, it was true, the camera is selective.

The implications were mind-boggling. I could pick and choose how I spent my valuable time, giving more of it to more important areas of preparation for air—or, frankly, staying in bed an extra fifteen minutes in the morning. I discovered I could use the camera, instead of the other way around. I had learned a secret to manipulating how other people perceived what they saw—even how I saw myself, how I made myself feel.

You know, of course, that manipulation is the basis of the entire cosmetics industry, the fashion houses, and magazines, and untold other business endeavors. And so it's appropriate that, in the same spirit of creativity and sneakiness, we use smoke, makeup, and mirrors every day to finesse our image as Baby Boomers. We're that wacky, wonderful, warped group of postwar offspring who saw nothing unnatural in leaning against the back fence on a still August day, eating a wholesome vanilla ice-cream cone, while we watched the guy next door with a Michelob, a Lucky Strike, and a pick ax digging a bomb shelter, a goddamn family-style bunker, while the missus was cheerfully fixing Sunday pot roast. We are the same generation of flower children who were nothing if not adaptable . . . who still can think wistfully of the '60s as a decade of peace and love despite the Vietnam War-that-wasn't-a-war; the assassinations of our president and his brother; the fiery deaths, on the launch pad, of three astronauts; and the hate-murder of a civil-rights leader. If we can put all of that into a unique, level-headed perspective that gets us through the night while we're bringing up our kids, memorizing pin numbers, formulating E-mail access codes, and debating paper or plastic, then *we can*, by God, figure out how to cheerfully blow off any mammal who would try to spoil the good times that we've been studying for all these years. It's up to *us* to take all that history, that perspective, that experience, those Zanax, and create the images of ourselves that make us feel comfortable. We need to feel comfortable enough to make the next years the most productive and mind-blowing of our lives.

In studying my friends' techniques, and reviewing my own, I have isolated a few favorites, which I share with you here. Feel free to modify the details and tamper with the system as you wish. After all, we are the trouble-making, unpredictable Boomers. Let's not let that PR go to waste.

- *Be Gentle with Yourself.* Never look in the bathroom mirror as soon as you get up. The shock could kill you. First, run a sink of good, hot water to put a nice coat of steam on the mirror. No sense calling the paramedics so early in the day.

- *If You Can't Beat Generation X, Confuse Them. It's Almost Too Easy to Be Fun.* When yet another twenty-one-year-old coworker with his hat on backwards, the little shit, asserts with an attitude that he's too young to know about Janis Joplin, bomb shelters, or the Kennedy assassination (either Kennedy), turn it around. Pull yourself to your full height and hiss, "Stop complaining . . . it's not *my* fault you missed the '60s! And anyway, what *wasn't* before your time, you lowest of whining, lazy, mouth-breathing, bottom-dwelling, carbon-based life forms?" Then grab his hat and slap him with it till he bleeds.

- *Cardinal Shopping Rule.* When you try on something you love, do not consult a three-way mirror more than once. If you like it, go with it. *You* never see yourself from the back, and what other people see is their problem.

- *If You've Got It, Use It for All It's Worth.* If you spend time working out and you watch what you eat, and the result is a body you're quite proud of, for God's sake don't present yourself to the world in baggy pants and big, oversize tops accompanied by hair that's teased till you look like Don King. It screams "I do all my shopping at Walmart because that's where the Gun Club Wives update their camo wardrobes."

- *Get a Chocolate Thrill.* When you can see that working out and dieting are paying off, wear something especially flattering to the mall and approach the Godiva chocolate counter. Do a little "I'm too sexy for my shorts" walk, and order a single piece of something rich and fattening, pointing out that today you're having only one instead of the usual half dozen.

- *Keep Having Fun.* If you always enjoyed listening to music and sipping whatever on Friday night, instead of going to bed early or feeling like you had to go out and raise hell, then do it now, alone or with the person of your choice. And allow yourself to get the same kick out of it that you did when you were young and stupid and had lower blood pressure because you didn't know all the nerve-racking things that you know now. I still giggle when I think about an exceptionally challenging Friday night on the air—the kind of night when you're glad you have tapes of the good ones, in case the company decides you're too freaky to allow back in the building—a night when anything that could go wrong did go wrong. I came home with the intention of working out and then rubbing Bombay Sapphire martinis all over my body, to try to forget. I suddenly realized I already had worked out that day, so I proceeded directly to those smooooth martinis in which big, blue-cheese-stuffed olives were marinating and calling my name. Actually, they'd been calling my name since 8:00 P.M. when we lost a live interview, an important piece of videoplaying digital equipment, and several scripts. Next thing I knew, it was 3:00 A.M. and I was waking up in front of the fireplace,

Sinatra still crooning "Angel Eyes," as I picked up the CD remote control and tried to switch off the fire. When something that brain-dead happens, laugh about it, just like you did on those crazy nights when you were twenty and stoned and trying to insert your door key into the button on the elevator in the apartment building of a friend whose face you no longer can recall. Remember how it felt when that lady with the blue hair who was perfectly straight was standing beside you, watching the whole performance, and you were trying to act cool and nonchalant? That's funny! Allow yourself to laugh over the silliest things.

- *Be in Love.* Doesn't matter whether it turns out well or not. Doesn't matter what you do about it. Just be in love. Keep those juices flowing. Be under the influence. Don't worry about tomorrow, as long as you're looking out for yourself today. Anyhow, all we have, all anybody ever had, is today; tomorrow isn't even a promise. Surrender to *l'amour.* There are worse things, and rest assured you will find them. Today, just enjoy that sweet, tender trap.

- *Keep That Public Image Going.* When you're going out with the grandkids, bribe them before you leave the house to call you "Mom" loudly in front of other people.

- *Loosen Up!* Now that you have the kids, the house, the golf clubs, the Volvo/Mercedes/Jeep Cherokee/BMW/Buick, the job, could you just loosen up a little? God, you're so uptight. Try this: Escape without stepping out the front door. Declare your independence from time and geography. Set your watch to the local time of your favorite place. Mine's been on European time for a year. I'm constantly having to count six hours back, but that's the fun of it. It reminds me of all the times I looked at that watch in little cafes, at the museum, while taking in the warm, springtime sun on a chair in a public *jardin*. And anyway, it's the *minutes* we count most these days: five minutes late, ten minutes early. Plus, if you're having an off day, you always can fudge a little and explain that you just got back from Berlin/Hong Kong/ the English countryside/Provence/Poughkeepsie, and haven't had a chance to reset your watch. The little white lies that are so easily forgiven are good for the soul. Why should kids have all the fun?

- *Holdovers from the '60s and '70s That'll Hold You Over.* Transcendental Meditation, here it is again. Remember when you and a friend split the cost of the TM classes, so that she could go and then come back and tell you all about it? You were so worried that her mantra, the one they told her was so sophisticated and specific, wouldn't work for you. Little did you know that "ohmmmmm" would work just fine for you and for most of the rest of the planet.

  Medication—*hey* now! The whole country used to be on a Valium jag. And certain people did smoke grass in the '60s and '70s. Who can forget those classic moments when you found yourself in the car driving home at two in the morning, breaking four blocks early for a red light? These days, it has been suggested that the herbal mood elevator, St. John's Wort, could replace Prozac as the legal substance most likely to keep Americans from getting twisted when we find ourselves *again* caught in traffic, long checkout lines, telephone trees, and other frustrating situations that are the by-products of our "advanced society." It may be St. John's Wort— or that tricky herbal combination of valerian, hops, and skullcap—that allows us to get a few hours' sleep, as we drift off at night with the aggravating image of that damned Windows 98 "hourglass" turning over and over, telling us to WAIT AGAIN for something.

- *Massage.* And then there was . . . Rolfing, a sort of legal mugging, a very deep muscle massage that could leave you bruised and having to explain to your boyfriend what the hell happened to you. You don't have to go that far this time; but a weekly, full-body massage will do wonders for your psyche and that body you've grown to love. And it doesn't have to cost an arm and a leg. Massage schools give great price breaks, and recent graduates will go out of their way to lure clients with low prices, soft lights, and as much Enya as you can take in an hour. In fact, I may have proof that massage is so good it's a religious experience: There is a viewer who likes to write me letters explaining the nuances of the full-body, baby-oil massage he would like to give me, and without fail he signs every letter "Love in Christ." So there must be a connection.
- *Test Your Baby Boomer Achievement Level.* Do you have

reading glasses stashed in every room of the house? Or did the prescription the opthamologist gave you just really piss you off? If we can't ignore changes in our eyesight, we certainly can make them interesting. Most of us have to face this at some point, and you can let it tear you up or you can have a little fun. It's quite an adventure to watch some of us in my all-adult French class address the situation. Many of us who need reading glasses just hate to pull them out, even those of us who used to. I don't even take mine. I do make one concession: On class days I wear my regular, clear contact lenses, not the colored ones whose lovely amber/violet/green opacity tends to roam around in one's eye, occasionally moving onto the pupil. This makes fine print more of a challenge than it ought to be, and my participation more entertaining than I'd like it to be.

As your eyesight changes, friends can take the pressure off. When I feel I am about to become aggravated with having to adjust to this, I remind myself that my friend Valerie has been wearing reading glasses since she was fourteen. And she likes to point out that fictional TV character Murphy Brown relies on them, too. She has been hunting for a pair like Murphy's for years. And Renate has the advantage of looking like a little German schoolgirl no matter what she wears. Her reading glasses have thin wire rims that hold little, blue-gray tinted, round lenses that give the impression that she's wearing them only for the hell of it, and that any particular vision improvement is purely incidental. Another career woman goes to Loehmann's and stocks up on those five-dollar-a-pair "designer" glasses with standard corrections, and spreads them around the house. Of course, she takes them from room to room as she's using them, and eventually they all wind up in the kitchen or the laundry; but she feels this is better than getting bored with one expensive pair, which she eventually will sit on or lose.

Here's yet another solution: position interesting-looking magnifying glasses on tables, desks, and bookcases. How lucky that they just happen to be around when the phone book needs reading, or the newspaper, or the fine print on that winning lottery ticket. They also save guests embarrassment when they can't see a damn thing any better than you can, and are every bit as reluctant to haul around glasses as you are.

• *How's the Memory?* Name three Leslie Gore songs. Name three of Rod Stewart's girlfriends. Name three Kennedys not in politics. Okay, two. Where *did* you put the house keys? There's nothing wrong with forgetting a thing or two, with all the things we have to remember. I don't care what the scientists say about our using only a quarter of our brains and that we should be better about it. My friends and I are every bit as smart as the scientists, and we have decided that if we could use any more of our gray matter, we would. It just so happens that humans do not come equipped with Pentium chips for faster processing, and all available memory is tied up with keeping track of license plate numbers, drivers license numbers, social security numbers, passcodes and passwords, telephone numbers, pin numbers, new area codes, parking space numbers, frequent flyer numbers, business-trip hotel room numbers, birthdates, expiration dates, due dates, and date dates. Then there are the number sequences we try to commit to memory, so that we can bypass those damn telephone trees that demand that we enter still more numbers, robbing us of our individuality and our right as consumers and taxpayers to talk with a real human, when all we want is a little information, or to get something fixed, or to give our business to somebody.

Those of us who have spent a Saturday afternoon or two mulling over this concept, with the help of a margarita or two, have concluded that the more aggravated we become over all this silliness, the less available memory we all have. And it naturally follows that the more aggravated we become, and the less memory we have, the less we care about remembering anything at all. This is a defense mechanism, and when it kicks in, the phenomenon known as "IOEOTO" (pronounced eye-oto) takes over, to keep us from vapor-locking and losing all ability to function. IOEOTO stands for "in one ear, out the other." Try to imagine a hollow length of tissue that connects the ears and runs through the memory portion of the brain. If it were a highway it would be a bypass of the business district; if it were plumbing it would be a strip of PVC with an overflow valve. This does not show up on X rays, and you really don't care, do you, because you know it's there. You've seen it work. When you think you can't retain one more concept, one more name or number, you switch on the bypass, open the valve, and let the rest just go by. We do, however, have an override mechanism that enables us to accept new information if we deem it extremely important while dumping something less useful to make room for it. Hence, you can see how you can remember your new boyfriend's cell-phone number, but can't recall your old boyfriend's shoe size. You have your priorities.

With this background on how humans cope with information, it is easy to understand that we can't blame ourselves when we have to write things down in order to have them when we need them. It has nothing to do with age stealing anything at all. It's just that the longer you're on this planet, the more you're exposed to. When all you had to remember was what time to be home from school, and how many pairs of gym socks you owned, you still had to write down your homework assignments. Look at it that way, and you realize how really well we all are doing.

Yet, there are ways to offer yourself some help, making you look even better, so good that twenty-four-year-olds who can't find the car keys will be jealous. First, consider hiding *their* car keys. It's beneath you, but it gets you started. Proceed to a devious scheme to remember more than one password. Make a sentence, using the words in the order in which you will enter them. Say you're at the office and you want to use different access codes for your computer log-on and your E-mail. Computer log-on: "w-o-r-k." E-mail access: "s-u-c-k-s." There you are. You'd be expected to use the same code for both; but your fingers will fly across the keyboard hitting obviously different sets of keys, impressing anyone who might be watching. And while no prying info-thief is going to figure that one out, you'll never forget it.

You can choose a word that has special meaning to you, like "yoga" or "beach." I'd stay away from foreign words, unless you really know what you're doing. A guy I know was studying German and he used the word that means "one." Unfortunately, Germans have so many ways to say "one" that it gets very confusing, and you might conclude it's no wonder so many wars go on over there. He forgot which "one" he was after. He tried "ein," then "eine," then "einer," then "eines," finally "einem." As you know, you usually get three tries to enter a voice mail or ATM password, then the system reprimands you like a seven-year-old and slams your butt into Technological Neverland, and you may or may not get another chance to try again. Should this misadventure happen at the ATM machine on a chilly evening of the ski vacation you saved a year for, you will be up the creek in Innsbruck when the machine eats your card. *You* can forget about eating until the American Express office or the bank opens in the morning.

- *And That Cute Little Shape of Yours:* Can you still get into your bell-bottoms? Do you still want to? (My God, you mean you *saved* them?) I say, good for you. Nowhere is it written that because you're over forty, you have to dress like Margaret Thatcher. No disrespect to Maggie, that's her thing. But the next time you try on a suit for business, look in the mirror at the store and ask yourself if there's any way you could be mistaken for a head of state or a UN delegate. If that's what you're going for, then knock yourself out, but if it makes you look like a teacher at a British boarding school, that translates to "less than appealing." If "boring" is not what you're about, if there's a spirit in you that feels exactly the same as it did the year you graduated high school, then why should you go out of your way to look as if you've lost it? I remember the day I went to work in an absolutely gorgeous, pink nubby suit with a straight skirt and a short, collarless jacket with braid at the edges and a blouse with a big bow at the neck. Someone told me with the most flattering intentions that I looked as if I had just come from a cabinet meeting. I felt . . . odd. I went home and looked at myself for the first time really objectively in that suit, and I saw a hairsprayed helmet-head in an outfit that made me look like Queen Elizabeth, not Coco Chanel. If the skirt were to be that far below my knees, then surely the heels should be higher and thinner. And the bow . . . forget about it. I shortened the skirt and it didn't help. I changed the shoes, and that didn't help. No other blouse really went with it. And I admitted defeat; I had worn this suit because, long after I fell out of love with it, I remembered it had been expensive. But it wasn't me, so I gave it away.

Do yourself a favor. Get out every piece of office attire you own and put it on in front of a full-length mirror and try to be as objective as you possibly can. Ask yourself if it's "you," the you that you feel inside. If it isn't, then fix it, change it, or get rid of it. It's better to own four things that are uplifting (you certainly can play around with them to make them different from time to time) than a closetful of clothes somebody else thinks you should be wearing.

Away from the office, dare to dress like you mean it. Make a solemn promise to yourself that you're not going to give in to the easy, mature American woman's way out of putting on sloppy clothes to go to the store. Warm-up outfits are for warming up; they're for exercise or for after. They are not for going to the drugstore or the lumber store or the supermarket. It doesn't matter that you're just running out for one or two things and won't be gone long. Aren't you worth more than that? It's such a cop-out, such a way of putting very little effort into getting yourself together. To throw on the "grubbies" is to give the impression that you don't have the energy that younger females have, to put on real slacks or a skirt and a nice little top and shoes that flatter you. Really, *aren't you worth more than that?* If you have to, take the extreme step that I did: Throw out the sweatshirt and sweatpants, just throw them out. Or tear them up to use as rags. Whatever you do to them, make it permanent. If you want something long to work out in, get leggings and promise yourself you'll get in shape and stay in shape to look good in them while you train, instead of hiding your form. Then, you won't have those ugly things to put on when you're just going out for a minute, and you'll be forced to treat yourself better.

The first time you're in the store and you forget your new attitude, and you happen to see your reflection in jeans and flats or clean sneakers and a top that makes you look great, you'll smile and thank God you decided not to go through the rest of your life just sliding by. And you'll walk like you're twenty years younger because—let's say it again—age is an attitude, and a number.

Every few months, reassess your makeup. Remember that less generally is better. Read magazines and, if you can do it without getting arrested or slapped down, when you see a woman who reminds you of yourself and has the look you want, really try to analyze what it is that makes her look that way. Maybe it's the way she does her eyebrows, or the shine in her hair. Maybe it's her walk or the way she outlines her lips. And if she's wearing a lipstick shade that just knocks you out, or a perfume you adore, she probably will be very flattered if you just out-and-out ask her about it; if she isn't helpful, you haven't lost anything. I once followed a woman around a store unabashedly trying to get a good look at the hair products she was carrying, and the lip pencils, because I wanted them to do for me what they did for her. I didn't really care who saw, because what I had to gain outweighed what other people thought of me.

- *Above All, Remember the Motto of the Baby Boomer*, that proud postwar product of the American fighting spirit of dedication, ingenuity, and determination:

NEVER GIVE IN, NEVER GIVE UP!

To Be Strong

There are so many aspects to being a strong enough person to do what you have to do, as independently as possible, to not let other people place limits on your dreams, and to accept responsibility for your actions. The key word is "independent." This does not mean you have to do everything yourself. That would take too much of your valuable time, and it would sap your energy. Choose your independent times. A woman once suggested to me, and it makes perfectly good sense, that when I have a carry-on bag to lift into an overhead compartment on a plane, and a man offers to do it for me, I should be delighted. Certainly I could do it myself. I probably lift weights more often than he does—but I don't feel the need to make a statement, when it means that I could break a nail. On the other hand, if life requires—as it did—schlepping my four-year-old to work with me at a Miami radio station at 5:00 A.M. (I went on the air with news and talk at 6:00), changing his clothes during the 7:00 network news, and giving him his hot oatmeal during Sports before I whisked him off to preschool during the fifteen-minute CBS Morning News with Charles Osgood, then I'm there. And you, of course, are equally capable—maybe more—of doing what you have to do. I believe most women have an extraordinary amount of inner strength, allowing them to accomplish amazing feats, day after day, without even realizing that they are doing anything unusual. They are just doing what they have to do.

Strong women seem to have two things in common:

1. They tend not to have much of an ego.
2. They enjoy the support of one or two good female friends who also are strong.

These women without big egos who do not consider themselves anything special, often are eager to share their thoughts on success and their personal experiences with other women who show a sincere interest. They do not jealously guard their secrets; rather, they hardly consider them secrets and are surprised that their experiences are of that much interest to other people. The things they share can be a tremendous inspiration to other women who have the desire and the drive to succeed, but need to know that the difficulties they are encountering are not unique to them.

Please note that there is a difference between having a big ego and giving yourself credit, which so often is just what you need to take the next step toward fulfilling your promise. Sometimes being able to acknowledge our successes—especially those accomplished under adverse circumstances—is what keeps us going. Don't be Mother Teresa. It's okay to pat yourself on the back, giving more credit anywhere you choose. *We owe this to ourselves.* But here's a bit of advice for every single one of us: If you think you've done what no one else can do, you're correct in concluding that you're very good and you've done yourself, your mom, and your high school principal proud, *but* you're no better a woman than anyone else. *Get past it.*

So much for ego.

Now, to that close friend who lends support. Often she does not live nearby. She may be hundreds of miles away, and your long-distance phone bill reflects the seriousness of the crises in your lives—the 2:00 A.M. depression calls, the 6:00 A.M. panic calls, the midafternoon advice calls, the evening anxiety calls. Then there are the cell-phone calls from the expressway that begin with, "I know you're at work and you're busy, but I just need to ask you something" or, "I need for you to tell me if I'm completely nuts." This person is such a good friend that she won't hesitate to tell you, "Yes, you *are* nuts," if she believes that and knows that honesty is what you need.

One of the best things about having a good friend is that when you don't want advice, you have the option of simply unloading everything that's making you crazy onto someone else's shoulders, and then just hanging up or walking away. You can launch into an "I'm going to do this" or "I'm going to do that" harangue, knowing full well when it's over that you've just saved your career or your relationship with Mr. Wonderful by not saying those things to the actual intended target. For such services the good friend could command a high price, but all she asks is that you be there for her when the time comes.

Hopefully, you are fortunate enough to be part of such an

enduring friendship. If you are not, it may be because you do not feel comfortable opening yourself to someone else—to another woman. I was there, and I have wondered why. Maybe the need wasn't strong enough. You certainly don't have to confide in anyone with whom you do not feel comfortable; but I believe you owe it to yourself to at least be open to the possibility of sharing a concern now and then, and seeing how it turns out. You may be watching a friendship shape up as your blood pressure goes down.

A successful business acquaintance says the biggest secret to taking control of your life is learning to say "no." This is especially difficult for women, because we are nurturers. We feel a *deep need* to meet other people's needs. It would be nice if we could confine this to our children, for whom nature intended it, and keep it separate from our other reason for helping, which is a conscious desire to please. That motivation ought to be the one that propels us toward late days at the office doing favors for colleagues, and those all-day baking marathons before the in-laws arrive. But somehow we seem to get it all confused. We feel a need to do everything for everybody.

We reason, when we begin, that if the task becomes overwhelming and we experience near meltdown, at least we can say we tried. How amazing that we should be willing to jeopardize our physical and mental health, when we wouldn't hesitate to advise anyone else on this road that she's doing too much and ought to back off. We place ourselves in jeopardy again and again, cheerfully taking on tremendous stress, and giving to the first taker the precious private time we need so much. Then we look in the mirror and wonder why we have circles under our eyes and we don't recognize the person staring back at us. We somehow feel that if we aren't doing all that's asked of us—meetings at work, plus phone calls for charity, taking the neighbors' kids for the afternoon, ironing his shirts, preparing a dish for potluck, having the Joneses over this Saturday because they can't make it next week—then we aren't doing our job and being good little girls. An amazing aspect of this is that many of the people we're so worried about offending would understand completely (especially the women) if we declined with a simple explanation. They might not like it, because the ball suddenly is back in their court, but you have made your decision and the problem no longer is yours. I'm reminded of a woman who typically kept long, regular hours at the office, and was awakened at one in the morning by her husband who was packing for a business trip. He complained, "I don't have any clean shirts." She pointed toward the laundry room, and went back to sleep. What was she supposed to do at that hour, that he couldn't do? She didn't feel guilty, because she knew that she didn't own the problem.

It's the guilt that gets us. And women agree that we also feel we're letting ourselves down as females, by not being able to take on all tasks. That's ridiculous. The first thing a businessman who is successful at time management will tell you is that he has figured out how to prioritize, placing the tasks he considers most urgent at the top of the list. If something at the bottom doesn't get done, then it doesn't get done; that's why it was at the bottom in the first place. And he has developed the ability to identify in advance the items most likely to be dropped from his day, and the nerve to tell whomever is asking that he or she probably is going to be out of luck. Women can learn to overcome their natural need to please everybody all the time, and handle things this way. It's like any other exercise: the more you do it, the easier it gets.

We also need to remember that each of us has a dear friend, a trusted, loving adviser always close at hand: ourselves. Have you ever considered offering yourself your own advice well in advance of the actual need, in the form of a written thought or two, tucked away in a secret place that only you know, a place like the ones where you used to hide little treasures when you were a child? There is such a place today; it's the safe deposit box. When I was thirty I began writing to myself, little comments and suggestions that I thought I might need in the future—instructions on keeping in touch with the "me" that I knew and liked so well as I was writing them. I was my own best friend. I would jot down—and still do—little reminders of life as it was then, the things that were important to me, the way I did my makeup, the things I knew about making myself happy, my daily routine, little secrets I shared with no one else, little giggles. My theory was that as life got crazier and more hectic and my priorities changed, I might forget the small joys that meant so much to me, the small rewards that always made me feel so good. Hell, I might forget that if you're still wearing your eyeliner the same way for five years, you'd better snap out of it, because that means you're getting stale in lots of other ways, too. And what better way to bring your special little secrets into the present—whenever they are read—than to give them to yourself in a sealed envelope. And so my safe deposit box holds them today, envelopes marked "Love Notes to Myself" at various ages.

When I decided to open the first one a few years later, I approached it with trepidation because I wasn't sure what I would find. Would I see a stupid person with an obvious intellectual void, a Twinkie? A woman with dreams that didn't come true? Not likely, since I don't do a lot of dreaming, though maybe I should. But was I about to take a blissfully ignorant psyche and plunge it into a depression of historical proportions, because I thought I had a great idea that turned out to be devastating? Well, here's the punchline, the best part: I actually missed opening the first one on time, because I was too busy *living and discovering and trying new things!* Isn't that just the best news? And when I finally did open it, I discovered that the things that were important to me when I wrote it still were important, though I had forgotten to give them enough time . . . like watching clouds go by, spending time outdoors doing absolutely nothing. Other cultures have elevated this to an art form, and for some reason we just don't get it. We Americans eat too fast, walk too fast, and make love too fast.

Let's do something about that, my friend. Today comes once. Let's clear little spaces for quiet moments with ourselves.

Go for It!

What did we learn today? We learned that life is weird. And unless you're sleeping facedown in the sandbox and not paying attention, you know it's totally unpredictable. Which ought to make us realize that there's no point in lying awake nights worrying about what might happen. You may have noticed that most of that doesn't come to pass; yet we just can't seem to turn off the natural, human urge to sweat it out. And no matter what we say, we really don't want to suffer alone. Even if you don't want to talk about it, it's kind of reassuring to have your partner toss and turn with you, just because there's that close connection between you.

One final exercise: Make a list of some of the worries that really took years off your life. Maybe some of them were worth it to you; but it'll be a real eye-opener when you see how often you could have saved yourself the anguish if only you'd known to treat things a little differently. Often, you can handle a situation with somewhat greater ease if you imagine the absolute worst that can happen, imagine what you would do about it, and then back off. Try it. You'll feel you're carrying a lighter load, because you actually will be.

Now that you've done that, take some good, liberating, deep breaths and smile and make up your mind that you're going to:

- Refrain from analyzing the life out of an experience. You can think things through until you pound them to dust, demolish the sensitivity, and suck the fun right out. Here's a little example that I experienced firsthand and remember to this day, because it was a lesson. When you do a television program over a period of years, you can go through lots of staff, especially at a truly remarkable company like Turner Broadcasting System. One of the reasons TBS did so well from the very beginning, was because employees had the opportunity to do just about anything they set their minds to, and were talented and hardworking enough to pull these ideas off. And of course once they did, they were gone to another department to try something else. So we had a parade of people producing our Sunday program, *CNN Week In Review*, and we always were waving them good-bye. One of them had the idea that if, when we pretaped the introductions to the reports, we did them over and over until they were absolutely perfect, it would be a good thing. My co-anchor, Bob Cain, and I did that, and eventually it really was perfect; but people are not. The world is not. Something that perfect is unnatural, and so unstimulating that if we hadn't had so much fun working together, we would have fallen asleep while we were doing it; it just wasn't right. We learned an important lesson: Perfection sucks. Just remember to keep that human element alive and well; if something feels good to you, it's probably exactly what you need.

- Dare to be different. When something appeals to you—a television show, a dress, a meal—it certainly isn't because it's the same as everything else. When you like it, you say, "I don't know what it is, there's just something different about it" not "Wow! I really love that because it's exactly the same as the last hundred and fifty of them!" That goes for people, too. Others are fond of you because you're who you are. Develop that and enjoy the process. They also are a lot more comfortable around people who are themselves. They may say they never would do what you're doing, but who cares—they're not you, and that's the point.

- Get out of your own way and have the confidence to take chances. No matter what the calculus teacher said in high school, you're not an irretrievably stupid person. You are fully capable of deciding what is and isn't worth risk. You knew, for example, that the satisfaction of supergluing that teacher's shoes to the floor was not worth the risk of getting kicked out of school the week before the prom. You know how much risk you can take. You know not to quit your day job to play the violin in the subway if you've got two kids and your hubby just had a fight with his boss. You could, on the other hand, start a small business in the spare room or go in with a friend to do the Web page you've been wanting to design, or take up rollerblading, or sneak off and work at the Pink Ponytail on your lunch hour.

- Understand that it's easier not to go it alone. Accept your friends' assistance and affection. Yet remember that even they won't always agree with you, so don't let it throw you when they try to help and you feel like they're putting you down. Real friends will be so concerned that they will take the chance of offending you by telling you the way they see it. They also will love you no matter what, admit when they are wrong, and comfort you without saying "I told you so" in those extremely rare instances when it turns out that you were the one who was wrong.

- Be prepared for the detractors—the ones who are not your friends and don't have your best interest at heart. If you dare to be different, they will come. Maybe they're jealous or resentful, or maybe in their tiny heads they really believe you're making a mistake. Be ready, and decide right now that you are not going to allow those people to make you doubt yourself. Like a bad TV show, turn them right off, because they're wasting your time. In a sense, you could feel flattered, because these people don't go out of their way to put down something that is not a threat to their dull perception of this wonderful world.

- Don't court adversity as a training exercise. I know this sounds ridiculous, but some people do, and they need to get help. I've been telling you that you should learn all you can about yourself, and I truly believe that, but it needs to be kept in perspective. Anyone who tells you that tremendous adversity is desirable as a character builder needs to be hustled from the room. Yeah, we want to learn, but we don't want to find out that much. I don't want to be a wise, nervous wreck when I die. If I have to choose, I'll take stupid, calm, and happy.

- Expect that not everything will go as planned. And when that happens, it is not failure; it's experience. Some things just are futile from the beginning and should not be attempted, even if you feel you have a God-given right to pull them off. An example in the most basic terms we all can understand: What girl hasn't tried to tinkle standing up? First, we do it because we don't see why not. Later, we resent having to disrobe just to get a little relief; finally, we're just thoroughly disgusted that our gender should need bathroom tissue when half the time there isn't any in the ladies' room, anyway. Yet we all have discovered that trying to do it standing doesn't work. This is an example of a doomed enterprise, and it should not be classified as failure.

  And who among us hasn't been in such a hurry that she tried to use the tissue before she was ready? These things ought to work, but don't. They just aren't meant to. Finding this out is what women call "experience."

Finally, if I have discovered one critical thing in this life. If one thing has entered my thick skull and stayed there, it is the truth that you absolutely cannot be anyone else; you really can't, so don't even try. You are blessed with a truly unique blend of talents and ideas . . . amazing gifts money couldn't buy . . . and you have a responsibility to be in touch with yourself to get to know what you're about and how best to make use of the special opportunity that presents itself to you with each new dawn. It naturally follows that you will want to help other people do the same. We'll never know it all, but then, the joy is in the trying.

This life is yours . . . embrace it!